THE ESSENCE
OF TRADE UNIONISM

The Essence
of Trade Unionism

A BACKGROUND BOOK

Victor Feather

THE BODLEY HEAD
LONDON SYDNEY
TORONTO

© Victor Feather 1963
Hardback ISBN 0 370 10276 2
Paperback ISBN 0 370 11367 5
Printed and bound in Great Britain for
The Bodley Head Ltd
9 Bow Street, London WC2
by William Clowes & Sons Ltd, Beccles
Set in Linotype Baskerville
First published 1963
New edition 1971

CONTENTS

Union Law 1815
Colliers Strikes 1824-26

ACKNOWLEDGEMENT

To the thousands of trade union colleagues at home and abroad who have
helped me, over many years, by talking
about their problems and listening to
mine, I am eternally and fraternally
grateful.

V. F.

Introduction

O NE definition of 'essence' is 'all that makes a thing what it is'. That seems simple enough. To set down in plain words all that makes trade unionism what it is is not so simple. The libraries are full of books on trade unionism. There are mountains of books on virtually every aspect of trade union work. Thousands of books, pamphlets and articles are published every year on this subject.

This torrent of words will go racing on because trade unionism plays a bigger part in every man's life year after year. Workpeople who are not themselves members of trade unions find that their own hours, wages and conditions are being set in relation to hours, wages and conditions negotiated by trade unions for their members. The salaries of professional men, like doctors and accountants and local government officials, have a relationship indirectly to the wages of miners, railway workers, and workers in the building trade. The pay of civil servants, whether negotiated with trade unions or not, takes into account the way in which wages are moving in outside employment.

In Britain, the pay of the men in the Army and the Navy and the Air Force moves upward as wages generally improve: since a corporal's pay is related to that of the private, and that of the sergeant to the corporal and so on, it is clear that even the pay of the Chief of the Imperial General Staff—and therefore his pension on retirement—is connected with what trade unions are doing.

When workmen get, through their union, a week's annual holiday with pay, the office staff expect to receive two weeks' holiday with pay because they always did have a week's holiday before. Not one of the office staff may be in a union, but the employer knows what they expect from him—and it happens.

In Britain there are nine million trade union members, yet the wages and salaries fixed on the basis of representation by unions apply directly to not less than sixteen million workers, and there are possibly another four million wage or salary earners who also benefit indirectly.

A 'fair wage' or a 'standard wage' is, often enough, another way of saying the 'trade union rate for the job'. Especially in those countries where 'standard rates' or 'fair wages' are laid down by the government as a legal minimum, it is not done without relation to some other standard. It is enacted in relation to the general standards of wages paid in industry or commerce which have been agreed between a number of employers and the trade unions to which workpeople belong.

So what trade unions do in a particular industry sends its ripples far and wide within the whole community. Many people in a higher-income bracket who have thought up to now that trade unions were suitable for manual workers or lower-paid groups, but not for them, are beginning to see that they are also necessary for non-manual and professional workers, if they are going to get proper recognition for the merit of their work. In many countries there have been trade unions for non-manual workers for years but they have not been strongly supported because of this attitude of mind. This attitude was sometimes the result of being closer to the management than to the workpeople in the factory. If the factory was small and employed few workpeople, the office staff was smaller still, and generally in day-by-day personal contact with the employer.

The modern development of industry and commerce

everywhere will be towards the bigger unit. Small firms will join up with one another to form bigger companies, or will be absorbed and taken over by bigger firms already in existence. Some offices in the United States, Britain, Germany, France and other countries have already become giant-size and have many hundreds or thousands on the pay roll.

It is not possible to fix the workers' pay and conditions of groups of this kind by an individually-negotiated contract of service for everyone. It can only be done satisfactorily by a collective agreement negotiated between the management and the workpeople's representatives, or, less satisfactorily, by looking at such an agreement made by another employer and adapting it. Without trade unions and the collective agreements they make with employers and employers' associations, modern industry would be in chaos. The closer that people work together in large groups the more need there is for wage standards and regulations, in the same way that people living together in large communities need more rules and by-laws than people living in isolation miles away from their nearest neighbours.

The wages standard which is most satisfactory is that which is negotiated to the satisfaction of both the management involved and the workpeople, and governments do well to keep this in mind.

Democratic governments usually have enough troubles of their own in keeping people satisfied in the civic and political spheres, without going into the wages field where nobody is ever fully satisfied with the result of the negotiations, since the employer would rather have paid less than what he eventually agreed to pay, and the union's claim was higher than what they finally accepted. There is always more satisfaction with a settlement which two parties themselves agree is fair than there would be on the part of either if the same settlement was made for them by the Government—a democratic government, that is. Totalitarian regimes do not have to worry until, of course, a revolution starts. Then they have real trouble.

It is not only in the field of wages and working conditions that trade unions are important. Their work and activities concern managements and affect industrial and agricultural output. Finance ministers are interested in this, too, because this is the source from which they and local authorities draw taxation, direct and indirect, to pay for all services which a modern community requires.

Where trade unions have been established, and that is almost everywhere, they have come to stay. Where they are not yet in existence, they will be. Where trade unions have been set up, but are not yet succeeding, they will succeed. Trade unions grow in hot climates and cold climates, in the east and the west, in the wet and in the dry. They can talk in any language, and in any kind of development. Literacy is an advantage but is not essential. Few workpeople in Britain could read and write when they formed their trade unions.

* * *

The idea of trade unionism is as old as mankind, and organised trade unionism becomes more highly developed as nations develop.

This book therefore tries to show what trade unionism is about, what it does. It is meant to be a kind of easy introduction to trade union activities and development, the purpose of trade unionism, its power, its rights, and its responsibilities not only to those who join but to the community and the nation in which it exists. Trade unionism is international, but that does not require it to be anti-national. Trade unions cannot be alien groups in any country. They cannot succeed in this way. They must be of the people, by the people, for the people.

In particular this book has the object of giving to ordinary working people of countries where trade unionism is new, a fair idea of what it is all about. School teachers in the villages and the new towns in countries where industry is new may find it helpful. Politicians and civil servants may find something of interest to them. Managements and employers in those countries may learn something from it which will give them a different view of what trade unionism means, and does, from that which they may have heard briefly elsewhere.

Professors and lecturers who give so much help in many countries at adult educational courses may find the book useful in parts for developing their own talks. One especial aim is that it may give useful help to active workers in young trade union movements who find themselves wrestling with problems with only a 'do-it-yourself' kit as a guide; they may find something in these pages which gives them an idea for a new approach or, alternatively, will give them added confidence if they find that what they have been doing is confirmed in the chapters which follow.

I

The First Hundred Years

It was the speedy industrial changes in Britain, starting in about 1760, which created the conditions in which trade unions began to grow. Before this time, the hatters, tailors and printers had established local trade unions or clubs in various towns but these were small and scattered. The shoemakers (cordwainers) of Norwich had even organised themselves into some sort of trade union group in the late 1600s, but there is no record of their continuous existence.

Trade unionism as we know it today, however, began with the growth of the factory system; the use of water power and, later, steam power, to drive the new machinery caused factory employment to grow and 'home' or 'cottage' industries to dwindle. The villagers had to move away from their cottage looms and benches to live in new towns which were being built quickly around a factory or a group of factories. These new towns consisted of row after row of small brick boxes for the workers and their families. There were no parks or open spaces, no clinics, hospitals or schools; only the most primitive forms of sanitation were provided, and cholera, smallpox and typhoid were common causes of death.

Men and women slaved night and day for a meagre livelihood. Children became wage earners at five years of age and were carried to work by their parents to toil twelve hours a shift, day or night. In thousands of cases, homeless and orphaned children worked, ate and slept on the factory premises; if they died at work, as many did, their bodies were thrown into a limepit kept open for the purpose.

In the newly-sunk coal mines, the picture was the same. In a Penistone (Yorkshire) churchyard there is a memorial to the victims of a pit explosion in the early part of the last century. The names of those killed underground are carved on the memorial. They include children of seven, eight and nine years of age. In the steelworks of north-east England and South Wales it was no different. For men and women, a working day was anything between fourteen and seventeen hours; the wages were no more than sufficient to keep body and soul together.

It was against this kind of background that the trade clubs began to grow. These were small and local, and the membership was confined to one trade or occupation. The members met at first in one another's homes, or secretly on the hillsides out of the town; later they met in the only meeting places available to them, the ale houses. They had discussions about their wages, hours and conditions, and also established their sick and burial funds and their out-of-work benefit fund, each man paying into the fund each week to help one another in distress.

Often the landlord of the ale house acted as their bank. Gradually the 'trade clubs' began to link themselves with their counterpart organisations in the district, and loose federations began to form. The stocking-knitters of towns in Leicestershire and Nottinghamshire formed a wider federation; the weavers in the West of England, the coopers in Glasgow, and the tailors in London followed suit. The hatters took a wider sweep and by 1771 had formed a national federation.

Employers at first, and later, successive governments, grew more apprehensive as these federations strengthened and developed. The echoes of the French Revolution and then a mutiny in the navy made them more fearful still. So in 1799, Parliament passed the Combination Laws banning trade unions, and making it illegal for any

13

group of workmen to combine together for any purpose relating to employment.

To give the Act an appearance of fairness, there was a similar ban on employers, but it was easy enough for two or three employers to meet socially without causing any comment, and there reach a 'gentleman's agreement' about wage rates and then impose these rates without fear of resistance from their workmen, as organisation was unlawful.

Nevertheless, workpeople did protest and resist. Many were prosecuted; savage punishments followed convictions and even as accused persons they were treated as felons. Perhaps because the enforcement of the law then was not very efficient, many unions continued their existence although with less open activity. In printing and brushmaking, for example, agreements were negotiated between unions and employers in 1805, and similarly in coopering in 1813.

It was not until 1824 that the Combination Laws were repealed, and during this quarter of a century of illegality, violence and lawlessness had become widespread. Long hours of work on the one hand, unemployment on the other, rising prices, low wages, bad housing, degrading living and working conditions, the demotion of skilled craftsmen to the ranks of the unskilled—all these had produced strikes, lockouts, resentment and, often enough, physical violence. Widespread and prolonged stoppages took place among cotton and wool textile workers in 1808, the Northumberland and Durham miners in 1810, and the Scottish weavers in 1812.

Machine-smashing by workmen known as 'Luddites', followers of a mythical King Lud, started in 1811 in the hosiery factories of the Midlands and swiftly spread to other parts of the country. This was a violent protest against the new machines which were putting large numbers of people out of work. Troops and militia were brought out to quell the riots. Some workers were hanged, others sentenced to transportation to Australia.

Yet nothing could stop the smouldering indignation and resentment with which workmen protested against their degradation. Workers in one trade and another began to give money and other kinds of sympathetic support to other unions in entirely different industries. They were recognising the struggle as a common cause.

Meanwhile other influences were at work, and circumstances were changing. The Press, public meetings and reform societies became critical of the government and anxiously demanded modifications in the law about trade unions, being fearful that the situation would deteriorate even more. Swifter services for correspondence and express stage-coaches were making it easier for contact to be made between trade unions over a wide area; news of victories and defeats and trade developments travelled faster and wider. Therefore organisation on a wider basis than a local centre became possible.

The repeal of the Combinations Laws in 1824 was followed the next year by an Act which gave legal recognition of the right to combine for collective bargaining and the right to strike; it was no longer illegal for a workman to pay contributions or levies to a trade union.

The 1825 Act in effect marked the beginning of the legal history of trade unions in Britain, although it was still difficult for a union to go about its normal business without coming into conflict with the law; this in fact was to remain the case for another fifty years. Immediately the 1825 Act was passed the local societies and clubs came out into the open; new societies sprang up and a great drive for membership started. National unions, formed by the amalgamation of local clubs, came into being to give one another greater strength to defend their wages. The spinners, the potters, the builders and the iron and steel shipbuilders were all among the early national unions.

The idea of 'one big union' to which all workers would belong, whatever their trade, was soon being proclaimed. Robert Owen, better known as the founder of the co-operative movement, formed the Grand National Consolidated Trade Union in 1834; within a year it was dead and buried. Badly administered and torn by differing factions it had little enough chance: but its main defect was that it had little basis for common action or common interest among the conflicting trades of its diverse membership.

Although trade unions were now legal, the authorities were still apprehensive about their growth, and many subterfuges were used to bring peaceful trade unionists before the courts. Peaceful picketing was described as molestation, obstruction, intimidation and threatening behaviour; heavy punishments were inflicted on workers by magistrates whose social and economic interests were on the side of the landowners and the employers.

The six men of Dorset, or the Tolpuddle martyrs, for example, were sentenced to seven years' transportation in 1834. As farm workers, they openly formed a union branch as they were lawfully entitled to do. They also adopted in their rules a solemn oath of brotherhood. It was this so-called 'secret oath' which was the pretext for the charge laid against them. Although great protest demonstrations were organised by trade unionists calling for a retrial or a pardon, it was not until 1838 that the free pardon eventually brought them back from Botany Bay, half-way round the world, to which they had been transported.

The next ten years saw the spotlight switched from trade unionism to the Chartists, whose charter aimed at universal male suffrage, and other reforms for parliamentary representation. Many trade union leaders in the south identified themselves with Chartism, but not those of the north and as Chartism began to falter, a trade union revival began. By 1845, the national unions of potters, spinners, tailors, printers, boilermakers, shoemakers and others were relatively strong. A miners' association of Great Britain and Ireland had been formed in 1841 but this had faded back into its former district associations by 1848.

Meanwhile, the emphasis of the unions on improved wages and working conditions had continued, but educational activity was also being thought about as a means of fitting trade union members to help themselves more. Alongside the motto 'Defence, not Defiance' was running a new slogan, 'Knowledge is Power'. The too-ready use of the strike weapon was being doubted.

In 1845 at a London conference of the various trade unions, there was talk of the 'mutual interests of employed and employer' and of the need for 'a good understanding between master and man'. Hasty violence was denounced and deplored. The Stonemasons' executive committee declared in a message to their members that strikes were a 'ferocious animal that you know would destroy you'. The unions had begun to look more positively at the problems of the day. They were talking about controlled apprenticeships, control of labour supply, and the maintenance of wages. They were also searching for more effective and stable organisation and membership. It was a further indication that unions had come to stay.

The first union to find the formula for success, based on a stable membership, a regular income, and an elected national leadership, was the Amalgamated Society of Engineers (now the Amalgamated Engineering Union). This was in 1851 when a number of district unions of engineering craftsmen pooled their assets and funds and began paying one shilling a week contribution to the new society. As their wages were between 24s. and 35s.

for a 58-hour week, this was a big slice out of their income.

The ASE started with 11,000 members and an income, therefore, of over £500 a week. It grew quickly. Out of this income it guaranteed to pay a fixed weekly benefit to members when they were sick, an old age pension when they reached seventy years of age, and a burial benefit to help a member's widow or dependants. In the next ten years, the ASE paid out £459,000 in sick benefits, compared with £26,000 in strike pay. It was also able to pay a full-time secretary, William Allan, and to employ a small staff in a central office.

The executive committee was elected by the members nationally and they exercised a central control. The local branches each had an unpaid secretary—who, of course, was a working engineer and a member of the union— and a committee elected by the local branch members from among their number.

Although the ASE followed a moderate line of policy, it was not welcomed by the employers and it had to fight hard for its victories. Its policy of paying a comparatively high benefit to members engaged in local strikes and lockouts made it a fighting instrument when that time came. This gave it great prestige among its members and drew admiration from other unions and respect from the employers.

The ASE took the principle of trade unionism wider than its own particular interest, too. In 1859 it gave £3,000 to building workers who were out on strike; its ability to do this impressed the various local carpenters' unions so much that they too formed their own national amalgamation in 1860. Naturally enough, they formed it on the ASE pattern and Robert Applegarth became its general secretary in 1862.

It was Allan and Applegarth, along with Coulson of the London Bricklayers, Guile of the Ironfounders, and Odger of the London Trades Council who exercised great influence in the 1860s. The Webbs called them the 'Junta', probably because this group's own description of themselves was the 'Joint United National Trades Association'. They stood for a policy of moderation, a procedure of negotiation, conciliation and arbitration in industrial relations, for providing self-help for their members through the union, for the accumulation and careful handling of union funds, and for a central policy and direction.

The old saying that 'money talks' was not out of their thoughts. They found that as unions became richer and more powerful, the employers' attitudes changed. Employers were more ready to negotiate with bodies which had both strength of membership and of finance.

2

The "New Unionism"

In the early 1860s, in the larger towns and cities of Britain, trade union committees were being formed, composed of the branches of all the unions in the locality. These were called the Council of the Trades of London, or Manchester, or Glasgow, quickly shortened to London Trades Council, and so on. Glasgow called the first national conference of all trade unions in 1864; but it was Manchester which convened, in 1868, the conference attended by 34 delegates representing 118,000 trade unionists which was in fact the birth of the Trades Union Congress.

About that time, in 1866–67, rulings in the courts had given unions a series of setbacks; in addition, a Royal Commission had been set up to examine trade unions as a whole. Only two of its eleven members could be regarded as friendly towards trade unionism; the chairman was an employer.

Nevertheless, the Royal Commission's report in 1869 was grudgingly favourable towards trade unionism although it recommended several severe restrictions. The 1871 Act followed, and its restrictions were opposed by demonstrations and the lobbying of MPs by the newly-formed TUC Parliamentary Committee. It is under this Act that trade unions may register themselves if they wish. This Act, along with the 1875 Act, gave the funds and property of trade unions some protection at law; it also gave them a formal recognition as important and legal bodies.

Up to this date, the trade unions had existed mainly for the skilled mechanics, craftsmen and men with a trade. The skilled men who emigrated from Britain in the 1870s and '80s because of unemployment took the idea of trade unionism with them and the unions they formed overseas were also organisations for skilled workers, i.e., craft unions.

By 1874 the TUC was over a million strong. Railwaymen, miners and agricultural workers had begun to organise. Trade unionism was broadening its base, but the unskilled were still unorganised.

The fierce trade depression during the next ten years saw the unions fighting a losing battle; as unemployment grew, wages shrank. The structure of the movement still held, however, and eventually a new breakthrough was made. This was in the field of trade union organisation for the lesser-skilled or general workers. The match girls of London formed their union in 1888; in 1889, the London gas-workers, led by Will Thorne, Ben Tillett and John Burns, won the eight-hour day. Tom Mann, Burns and Tillett followed up by organising a London dockers' strike for a minimum wage of sixpence an hour. With the help of public opinion, a great victory was won and dockers' unions sprang up in other ports. The seamen organised; small local textile unions amalgamated.

Teachers and shop assistants and clerks began to form their unions. The Miners' Federation on a national basis was formed in 1888 with 36,000 members; within five years this had risen to 200,000. A great boom in trade union membership was taking place, with women workers and non-manual workers beginning to play an important part.

From 1880 to 1900 there was a tendency towards centralisation. The substantial funds and national policies of the growing unions required the authority of an executive committee with national responsibility. The power of the branch to make local decisions had to be yielded in part to the national executive, for the funds of the union were derived from the members of all the branches and it was only a body responsible to all the branches, that is, a national executive, which could sanction the spending of these national funds on strike pay, unemployment, sickness and death benefits and other expenditure.

More business-like methods of administration became possible with a central authority, for an official in the full-time employment of the union could be expected to become more expert, knowledgeable, and proficient about matters affecting the membership; the local voluntary official who had his living to earn elsewhere could devote only his spare time to union affairs. The new group of full-time general secretaries still relied, of course, on the information passed through to them by the local branch officers, but the experiences reported from one branch could be usefully passed along to another branch later if a similar difficulty was encountered.

As the central office or headquarters became the pivot, so the members began to look towards the national leadership for help and advice. Comparisons of local and district wages agreements with employers became simpler. A demand for uniformity of wages and agreements grew and the seed of national negotiations and national minimum standards of hours, wages and conditions was sown. The great slump in trade which began in 1891 strengthened the move towards consolidation of authority in the unions as employers began to press for wage cuts.

Again over the years that followed the unions were fighting a rearguard action. The normal pattern of strike, starvation and surrender still prevailed, but the unions' resistance was strong and better organised, and in defeat they were unconquered.

A new and startling shock followed the slump. In 1901 in Taff Vale, a small mining town in South Wales, there was a railway strike, at first unofficial but later given the backing of the union. The Taff Vale Railway Company thereupon sued the railwaymen's union for damages, and to the general amazement of the legal profession was awarded damages in the enormous sum of £23,000. The effect of this judgment was that any union which then sought to resist a wage cut by striking was in peril of being sued and suffering heavy financial damages.

Between the Taff Vale judgment and the 1906 Act which remedied this situation, it was estimated that workmen lost £12 million in wages as a result of wage cuts to which they could offer little resistance. It was this judgment probably more than anything else that brought many unions to the support of the small struggling Labour Representation Committees. These committees pointed out that the voices of the employer and the landowner were both to be heard in Parliament, 'but,' they demanded, 'where is the voice of the labourer?' They went to work to get working men elected to Parliament. In the 1906 General Election, candidates sponsored by the Labour Representation Committee won 29 seats; on this result the Labour Party formally came into existence.

A further legal assault now had to be faced. In 1909 a railwayman named Osborne, a branch secretary of his union, asked the courts to stop his union spending funds on political action. He won his case, and this barred all unions from providing the young Labour Party with an income, or giving financial assistance to those of their members who had become M Ps.

It looked like another severe setback for the unions, but they fought to get the law changed. In 1911 an Act was passed providing that M Ps should receive a salary from the State for their duties, and this eased the position so far as working men M Ps were concerned.

In 1913 another Act was won by the unions which permitted them to establish a separate political fund in addition to their general fund, and to make payment from this fund towards political activity.

Meanwhile the unions had been invited into the administration of the new health and unemployment insurance scheme. They had had considerable experience in providing this kind of benefit. In fact, much of the data on which the Government scheme was based was derived from the records of those unions which had been providing such benefits for their members for almost sixty years. The prestige of the unions was growing.

The outbreak of World War I in 1914 called for a great national effort from industry and the response of the unions was patriotic. The 'triple alliance' of miners, transport workers and railwaymen had been formed just before the war, and although in the post-war years it did not measure up to the industrial trials it was to face, it helped to keep industry on an even keel throughout the war. Elsewhere there were difficulties, and strikes took place, mainly unofficial and sporadic and usually in munitions, on the question of the replacement of skilled workers by others of lesser skill and women, a process described as 'dilution'. In 1917, for example, $5\frac{1}{2}$ million working days were lost through strikes, mainly in the munitions industry, a big contrast proportionately with what happened in World War II.

The Trade Union Movement continued to grow strongly during the 1914–18 war. Its membership in 1915 was $2\frac{1}{2}$ million and in 1918 it had reached $4\frac{1}{2}$ million. The two principal causes of industrial disturbance during this period were the rising cost of living and the extension by employers of the dilution agreements. These agreements had been made with the unions to assist the introduction of women workers and lesser-skilled workers into more highly-skilled jobs in connection with the war effort. The employers, however, began to apply this dilution to other kinds of jobs, and many strikes took place to try to stop this breach of the agreement.

In an endeavour to find a solution to this serious war-time problem the Government appointed a committee, under the chairmanship of the Speaker of the House of Commons, Mr Whitley, to examine the future pattern of industrial relations; its report in 1917 led to the formation of a number of joint industrial councils in certain industries. In the civil service, too, such committees were set up, and there they are still known officially as Whitley Councils.

At the end of the war a bitter conflict developed between the unions on the one hand and the employers, aided by the Government, on the other. A railway strike took place in 1919 for wage claims which had not been pressed by the unions during the war. In 1920 a long strike took place in the mining industry. The miners suffered defeat, and wage cuts began to be imposed by employers in one industry after another. One effect of this was to bring the unions closer together, and a further amalgamation of engineering unions, forming the Amalgamated Engineering Union, was followed in 1922 by a score of unions amalgamating to form the great Transport and General Workers' Union, led by Ernest Bevin.

The Trades Union Congress was re-organised in 1921 so that it could give greater assistance to its affiliated unions; each union was placed in its appropriate industrial grouping and a General Council was elected, consisting of representatives from each of these groups and served by a full-time staff of experts at a London headquarters. Trade union membership, which had risen to 6½ million in 1920, was now falling as unemployment grew, and by 1925 the membership had gone down to 4½ million.

A further wage reduction and a longer working day threatened the miners in 1925, and they turned to the TUC for assistance. After months of effort to withstand this threat to the miners, a special conference of all union executives was summoned by the TUC General Council. This conference lasted from May 1 to May 3, 1926, and at the end of it the national strike call went out. For ten days, starting on May 3, all industry and transport in

Britain was at a standstill, except for work essential for life and safety.

On receiving assurances from the Government which seemed to make a compromise possible, the national strike was called off by the General Council on May 13. The miners held out for six months longer but finally a return-to-work order was given by the Mineworkers' Federation.

Because of the trade slump and long-drawn-out stoppages, the trade unions had been weakened. The Government at this stage brought in the 1927 Trade Union Act. This Act made it illegal for civil service unions to remain affiliated to the TUC. It made all 'sympathetic' strikes illegal—strikes, that is, called by one union to help another in a different industry.

Further, in an attempt to weaken the Labour Party, the Government altered the 1913 Act concerning the political funds of trade unions. This 1927 Act was bitterly resented by trade unionists, who regarded it an act of revenge for the national strike. It was repealed in its entirety by a Labour Government in 1946, although before then a modification of this had been discussed with the war-time Coalition Government.

The unions' bitterness in 1926–27, however, did not drive them into blind opposition. On the initiative of the TUC, talks were arranged between the unions and employers' associations to see if it might be possible to limit industrial disturbances and create a better atmosphere. Ben Turner, a textile union leader, was the chairman of the TUC and Sir Alfred Mond the leader of the employers. The Mond-Turner talks which followed helped to clear the air, although no formal agreements were reached, and laid the foundation of much modern trade union thought, principally that trade unions should have an interest in the efficient conduct of industry to the benefit of the nation as a whole.

The world slump which was already on its way gave

further point to this need. The clouds of unemployment and poverty thickened from 1929 onwards and policies began to be hammered out by the unions, through the TUC, to find out the principles by which Britain's basic industries could be developed to ensure full employment and planned to provide greater stability and a higher living standard. Better social security provisions were envisaged and great campaigns were organised by the TUC to publicise these programmes to the public generally.

Meanwhile the growth of Fascism was seen in other countries. The seizure of power by Hitler in Germany in 1933, which he followed immediately by crushing the trade unions so that he could obliterate democracy, had its effect on the TUC. The TUC repeated its condemnation of totalitarianism in any form. When war ultimately came in 1939, the TUC were able to pledge the unions to full support of the national effort against Fascism and aggression, demanding, too, that unions should be brought into full consultation by the Government on all changes likely to affect workpeople.

Joint machinery for consultation between the Government, employers and unions, was set up widely and quickly, and covering every aspect of civilian life. For six years the work of the TUC and the unions was directed almost solely towards bringing about a successful conclusion of World War II, making sure at every point that the voluntary sacrifices of democratic principle which the conduct of the war required would be fully restored at the end.

During this period the TUC also worked out a policy for the control of basic industries which they wished to see introduced when the days of peace returned. This policy emphasised that there was no single, rigid pattern of public control which could apply to all industries, and that not all the major industries needed to be nationalised. What was required in certain industries, the TUC said, was a sufficient measure of public control to ensure that the national need was served rather than the special interests of any particular group.

During the war, too, proposals were being prepared by the TUC for the revival of the international trade union movement, and to widen its membership; soundings were being taken for this new international development in 1944, twelve months before World War II came to an end.

The British trade union movement has always shown the greatest possible interest in the development of international trade unionism and sister trade union movements in all parts of the world know of the TUC's fraternal activities.

In 1945, the TUC membership had grown to $6\frac{1}{2}$ million. Its authority and influence had reached a new high level. Its prestige in the eyes of the nation was higher than ever before.

3
Structure and Objects

THE Trades Union Congress is the central body of the trade union movement in Britain. It has 9·4 million members who are organised in 150 unions.

The unions affiliated to Congress cover practically every trade or occupation or profession. There are unions for dockers, miners, bank clerks, civil servants, actors, journalists, railwaymen, bricklayers—everybody. The biggest union is the Transport and General Workers' Union. It has 1·5 million members, and is still growing.

These 9·4 million members are organised in the local branches of the 150 unions, and the branches may be attached to district committees. The district covers a number of local branches and the district committees are composed of representatives from each branch, elected each year. In turn the district committees may function under a regional committee which is composed of representatives from the district committees within the region.

In the TGWU the regional committees elect 24 representatives to the general executive council of the union, the number from each region varying according to membership. Also on the general executive council are 11 representatives from what are called 'the national trade groups'. For example, a docker who is a member of this union may attend his local branch and take part in the union's general activity there; but, in addition, he may also attend meetings of the docker members only, to discuss matters which are of special interest to them but which may not affect other members of the union who are, say, road passenger transport workers or road haulage drivers.

Specialised sections are called trade group committees,

and their district or area committees are represented on the appropriate regional committees. In addition the regional trade group committee is linked with its national trade group.

The members of the branch committees, including the branch officers, are unpaid, and follow their normal occupations during working hours, giving up much of their spare time in the evenings and at weekends to carry out union work. The members of the district and regional committee are also unpaid, but as the decisions that they take involve a great deal of work the regional secretary is a full-time officer and has other full-time officers to assist him. These other officers serve the various district committees and the regional trade groups and are responsible for advising the members, taking up those grievances which need more attention than the unpaid branch secretary can give to them, and doing other negotiating and administrative work.

Every two years the TGWU has a delegate conference. Delegates are elected by each branch to consider all matters relating to the conduct of the union. The report of the general executive, an extensive printed document, is sent to the delegates some weeks in advance of the conference so that they may study it, discuss with their branch any matter which should be raised at the biennial conference, and make themselves thoroughly familiar with the national picture of their union's activities.

The union's chief officer is the general secretary. He is elected by a ballot vote of all the members and is responsible for carrying out the decisions of the general executive and the biennial conference. He is helped by the assistant general secretary who is elected by the general executive after having passed a written and oral examination on the union's affairs conducted by representatives of the general executive council. All other officers are similarly appointed. The president of this union is elected by the general executive council, and this is not a full-time job.

As a contrast, in the Amalgamated Union of Engineering and Foundry Workers (which has almost a million members) every officer is elected for a limited period—now three years—and, of course, each is eligible for re-election. The president of this union becomes a full-time officer, and all the seven national executive council members, who are elected on a regional basis, become full-time officials automatically.

Each of the seven regions has a full-time secretary with an assistant, and within the regions there are full-time divisional organisers. The divisions themselves are made up of district committees, and in some cases, the district secretary also is a full-time officer. None of the branch secretaryships is a full-time job. All these officers report to their various appropriate committees, the branch secretary to the branch committee and the branch members' meeting, the district secretary to the district committee, and so on. These meetings are usually held once a month.

The national executive council themselves report to a national committee of 52 representatives elected from all the regions of the union meeting once a year. Naturally, between one annual meeting and another, the national executive council are reporting their decisions to the branches by means of circulars and meetings with the members, and by articles and information in the union journal.

In a union of, say, 2,000 or 5,000 members, although the structure and procedure of the union will naturally be different, the same principles apply. It will have local branches, varying in size from perhaps 20 members to 100. These members may attend a monthly branch meeting, presided over by the branch chairman whom the members have elected at an annual meeting. The branch secretary, also elected at an annual meeting, deals with the correspondence of the branch, and records the

31

decisions of each branch meeting; that is, he writes the minutes.

All correspondence for the branch, whether it is from the union head office or any member or from any other source, should be sent to him so that it can be placed on the agenda of the branch meeting for a decision on it to be made. The branch secretary may also be responsible for dealing with the branch register of membership, ensuring that the weekly contributions which the members pay are properly recorded. He will be responsible for sending the union benefit for sickness, or unemployment or accident to the members.

In some cases, the member will pay his contribution at the branch meeting; mainly he will pay it each week to one of his fellow-members at work who may act as a union collector for perhaps 10 or 20 other members. The collector marks the member's card with the amount he has paid and the date on which he paid it, and passes this money along to the branch secretary, so that the details of each member's payment are properly entered in the branch books.

In a union of 1,000 members there will probably be only one paid official, the general secretary, and he may be only a 'part-timer', doing union work part of his time and otherwise following his normal occupation. A union of 5,000 members may have three full-time officials; that is, a general secretary and two organisers. The other officers, such as district committee secretaries, may receive a small payment—an honorarium—of perhaps £10 or £20 a year.

Virtually the whole local activity of trade unionism in Britain is on the basis of voluntary work by the union members. The 9·4 million members are organised in roughly 40,000 branches, and only about 300 branch secretaries are full-time officials. The others receive an annual recognition of perhaps £10 or £25.

No branch chairman receives a salary other than perhaps a small token payment each year to show appreciation. There is no payment of branch committee members. If it were not so, trade union contributions, which average about fifteen pence a week, would have to be doubled at least. Even out of that contribution about fivepence is put on one side for provident benefits and part of the balance is put to reserve.

The pay of the full-time union officers in Britain may seem low in relation to the responsibility placed upon them. The practice, however, is that a man who leaves his normal job in industry to become an official of his union does so knowing that his pay from the union will be little higher than he had before, that his hours will be twice as long, and that his weekends will no longer be as free as formerly, since he is expected to be available in the service of his members day and night, seven days a week.

A man who becomes a full-time trade union officer knows all about this before he starts, for as an active member he will have already served the union in a voluntary capacity for several years and in this way earned the confidence of the members who have chosen him for full-time office. This background of voluntary work among the full-time officials and the branch officers is one of the characteristics of British trade unions; although many trade union officials would blush at the thought, they are, in fact, men dedicated to the service of their fellow men.

They have many problems, but they have never had the problem of a split trade union movement. In some countries the trade union movement is split into several rival parts on the basis of religion or politics and this leads to confusion among workpeople.

A workman is paid wages for the work that he does. He is not paid more wages by the employer if he votes for one party and less if he votes a different way. Nor is he paid more because he belongs to one religious faith instead of another. The payment of wages by an employer is a business transaction which has nothing to do with either politics or religion.

When the workman gets his wage and goes to the shops he is not charged more, or less, for his food on the basis of his religious or political beliefs either. That, too, is a business transaction.

Although trade union membership means more than a simple business transaction, the common link between the workpeople in an industry is that the wage is paid for work done, whoever is doing it. Therefore those who are doing it should act collectively in one union, and the union should be organised solely on the basis of the welfare of workpeople, regardless of their religious or political beliefs. Neither of these should be a qualification or disqualification for membership.

There can be disqualification of membership, however, on the basis of the conduct of the individual member; that is, if his conduct is helping interests in opposition to that of the union and its members, or is contrary to the union rules, or if his behaviour as a member of the union is likely to bring the union into disrepute.

The object of a union is to get the best possible living standard and working conditions for its members. Decent wages, good conditions of work and reasonable hours, with security, are its principal objects. On this basis, trade unions and employers' associations should not find it difficult to reach agreements which will be lasting and beneficial to both, giving stability of employment and regular output.

4
General Policy

THE main job of a trade union is to maintain and improve the living standards of its members. That, in a nutshell, is the only fixed principle of trade unions, wherever they may be. How they set about that work, however, cannot be fixed.

Trade unions by themselves do not decide the circumstances in which they work; they must do the best they can in whatever circumstances they find themselves. All kinds of considerations help to make these circumstances. The policies of governments in regard to industry generally is something which unions, as unions, cannot decide. International political developments are not determined by trade unions, although trade unions, like other bodies, can influence them, and are influenced by them.

The dismissal of a member by an employer creates a problem with which a trade union may have to deal, although the circumstances were not created by the union. It is not a union which creates a demand for higher wages, it is the desire of the members themselves, usually sparked off by increased living costs, which compels the union to open up negotiations with employers.

It is no use any union executive committee or official having predetermined views about the method of solving the members' problems. The procedure for dealing with industrial problems may be well established, but the argument which brought successful results on one occasion may fail miserably on another, because it is impossible to duplicate the circumstances exactly; nor is it usually the union which creates the circumstances, although it has to deal with them.

The living standards of workpeople in most countries are based on the workers' own wages. There may be other income from social security benefits, large or small, but basically the weekly or monthly earnings fix the standard.

It hardly needs to be said that the wage must be considered in relation to prices. A workman earning £15 a week is no better off, if a suit costs £15, than if he were earning £10 a week and the suit costs £10 and other commodities proportionately. So the living standard is not measured solely by the number of notes or coins in the wage, but on that amount of pay in relation to the price of the goods the workman needs in order to live.

If a union therefore is going to maintain and improve the living standard of its members, it will become involved in the consideration of all those factors which affect prices, such as the indirect tax which may be levied by a Government on foodstuffs or a direct tax on wages and incomes. A union must have something to say about this kind of thing because its members' living standards will be affected one way or the other. A tax on fuel used by 'buses or trains may mean that the employer will begin to look for savings in his running costs, and such savings may be at the expense of wages. Therefore the union cannot ignore the effect of such taxes, and would be entitled, probably in association with the employers, to protest about such a tax and call for its early withdrawal.

In addition to wages and prices, those Government policies which make for full employment or unemployment must be a concern of a union. If there is unemployment or short-time working in an industry, the standard of living of the members is altered although there may not have been, up to that point, any alteration in either wage rates or prices. The causes of such unemployment are bound to come within the consideration of a union acting in the interests of its members.

Sometimes it is said that unions should not concern themselves with politics, although in modern society, as governments become more and more concerned with industry, it is difficult to see how a union can do its fundamental job without keeping itself informed of government activity and making representations to a government about actions it takes which react against their members' living standards. Whether a union should specifically tie itself in with a political party is a different matter. A union should certainly avoid becoming dominated by any political party, for if it does that then its fundamental objective of acting where it can, and when it can, in the interests of its own members, becomes secondary to the interests of the political party which dominates it.

It is natural for a political party to wish to become the government and then to stay in power as a government, even though this may mean the subordination of others' interests. A bona fide party with a genuine desire to help trade unions will not want the unions to become the party cat's-paw, for that would be the quickest way to guarantee the enmity of other parties, and employers' associations, towards the union.

There are dangerous possibilities for a union which allows itself to become dominated by any party. It provides the possibility of internal dissension, and of some groups of members, who may believe that their interests are being sacrificed to help a political party, breaking away from the union and setting up a second 'independent' organisation. Industry itself will suffer because competing claims will be put forward by each union's leadership in an endeavour to either hold or attract membership. If a settlement is reached between one union and a management, the tactic of the other competing union is invariably to attack that settlement, although they themselves would otherwise have thought it acceptable.

Rivalry of this kind can lead to industrial stoppages which lead to loss of work and an ultimate lowering of the workers' living standard; in short, the opposite of what was intended. The most serious possibility of all is for workpeople to be led into strikes at the behest of a political party against a democratically elected government, solely for a political purpose.

In Britain, as is generally known, the Labour Party was originally formed by some trade unions, and the historical reasons for this decision are well documented. It was the particular set of circumstances at the time which led the unions to their decision, and it does not follow that other trade unions in other countries would find it necessary to take a similar step, or that they are ever likely to meet the same set of circumstances. If history and economic circumstances had been different, the Labour Party, as such, might never have come into being, and instead, there might have been a small academic Socialist Party without a mass membership, still striving to win popular support.

Whatever government may be in power, trade unions must be free to follow their collective policies, independently reached, towards their basic aim. They have an economic function in the industrial field, and must also keep an eye on political decisions by governments which may have a direct effect on industry and thus directly affect the living standards of trade unionists. The decision of a government to raise or lower the bank rate, or to change a tariff, or to levy a tax on prices or incomes could have the effect of changing consumer demand and thus affect the livelihoods of the workers engaged on the production of consumer goods.

On issues of this kind, political parties and individual politicians have set out quite deliberately to gain the support of trade unionists for specific objectives. In these circumstances a trade union, especially one which is still working hard to establish its position, has got to be on its guard. The job of a trade union leader is to look after the interests of his members, not to serve the purposes of other groups or individuals who see in the unions a pathway to political power.

It is in the nature of some politicians to use every means possible, providing those means are legal, to satisfy a personal ambition for political power: and when that power has been achieved, to use it in such a way as to perpetuate it, even if this should mean attacking and curbing the means whereby they originally secured that power. Every political situation should be judged on its merits, and only from the standpoint of the members' interest. The policy of a union must not be determined on whether it suits one political party or another, and even less should it be based on the personality of one Minister as against another.

It is in the nature of politics for groups and cliques to develop, particularly within successful parties: the nature of successful trade unionism is to avoid all cliques and factions and for decisions to be made in the interests of all, by democratic procedures. Ministers change and Governments fall, but the union must continue, for its members will continue to meet problems in industry whatever else may happen.

Trade unions which are independent—that is, whose decisions are made only by their membership, free of domination by employers, governments and political parties—are a true training ground for democracy and a better means of winning and holding improved living standards and better social provisions than election manifestos. If that is fully realised by trade union leaderships, they will concentrate their activity towards the service of the union in the industrial field, knowing that success in that direction will lead towards the establishment of the improved standards to be achieved through higher real wages, shorter hours and better working conditions; these in themselves will lead towards better housing, more educational facilities, and proper health and social security provisions.

In the course of attaining their principal objectives, trade unions must concern themselves with many other related matters. For example, while they must try to secure compensation for their members injured at work, they must also be concerned with steps to ensure the prevention of industrial accidents by the promotion of safety and accident prevention measures, the reduction of sickness by better ventilation, lighting and heating, the proper provision of canteen facilities, and so on.

Accidents at work are not only injurious to the individual who suffers but to his family who depend on his earnings and also the management who depend on his production and who are also concerned from a humane point of view about the individual's welfare. Compensation in money for a broken back or an amputated arm may be as much as can be done; it is better, however, if there are no broken backs or amputated arms.

Are goods stored properly or are they liable to fall and injure someone? Are the gangways and aisles kept clear or will someone, in trying to dodge an obstacle, fall against a machine, or a moving lathe? Is dangerous machinery properly fenced? Good and tidy 'housekeeping' in a factory is essential for safety. What about health provisions? Proper toilet and washing facilities can be more important than medicine. One may prevent, the other only cures. Can workers who bring their own food eat it in clean surroundings? Is the ventilation right? Does the factory get too hot, too cold?

All these can be subjects of joint consultation between unions and employers, and of course a thousand other matters which can arise in the employment of thousands of people.

Some of these matters are covered by legislation in many countries and sometimes it is thought that these beneficial developments came as a consequence of political action in the first place. That is not generally true. What is true is that in most cases the basis for the ultimate legislation was set out in the voluntary agreements and arrangements reached in industry between the organised employers on the one hand, and organised workers on the other.

In Britain particularly, legislation follows practices which have already become widely applicable, the intention of the legislation being to pull the minority of laggards into line with what has become the standard practice over a wide range of industry.

This concentration on practical matters, and an industrial approach to industrial problems, reflects itself in the kind of leadership which trade unions get. The leadership of every union in Britain is composed of men and women who are either still working in their own industries or, in the case of the full-time leaders, were themselves formerly employed in the industries they now lead.

The Transport and General Workers' Union is led by a former truck driver. The railwaymen, who are organised in three unions, one for engine-drivers, another for clerical staffs, and the third for railway workers generally, are led by former railway employees. An ex-joiner is the general secretary of the Amalgamated Society of Woodworkers, and former print workers lead the printing unions. Textile workers, dockers, miners, steel-workers, office employees are at the head of their respective unions. This is the principle which applies generally throughout British trade unions.

The advantage of this, of course, is that every leader has personal knowledge, gained through his own working experience, of the conditions of work of his members. Workers who listen to their leaders' speeches know they are listening to a practical man who understands the special problems and difficulties which arise from their work. Employers, too, know that when they meet such leaders in negotiations they are dealing with men, who like themselves, have a personal and practical background in the industry. They are more likely to respect the arguments such men put forward than they would the case argued, as it were, by a professional advocate briefed specially for the occasion.

This, too, is probably why trade union agreements negotiated with employers in Britain have such a practical appearance about them. There is no legal jargon in such agreements. They are kept uncomplicated, and written in a language which every trade union member can understand. It is not the object of either the trade union negotiator or the employer to word the agreement in such fancy language that only they can understand it. It is written in clear terms, so that when it is published it speaks for itself in a language that normal people have no difficulty in understanding.

If, in the event, it turns out that two different interpretations can be put on a clause in the agreement, that particular clause can be re-written and made clearer at another meeting of the persons who were the signatories of the agreement. No lawyers are used or needed, and there is no recourse by the parties to judges or the courts for an interpretation. Law is often a lengthy and expensive business in any case, and its results are never as satisfactory as a voluntary settlement mutually agreed between the parties involved.

About the only occasions on which trade unions use the legal process are when they are assisting their members to get compensation for injuries sustained by them in the course of their work; even so, the cases settled out of court outnumber court settlements by at least ten to one. In such cases, the negotiation is not undertaken by the unions' officers themselves: the work is usually passed over to a firm of solicitors which the union 'retains'—that is, the union either pays the solicitors a small annual 'retainer', in return for which the solicitors will handle all the cases that may crop up in a year, or alternatively the union may pay the solicitors a nominal amount for each case. Every union includes this 'legal benefit' in its recognised services to its members, and no settlement is made by the lawyers 'out of court' without the agreement of the union in consultation with the member.

5

Administration and Procedure

A LOCAL trade union leader who works full-time for a union will never be able to live in luxury; nor for that matter will a district or national leader, both of whom are paid a little more because of the greater responsibility they carry.

The pay varies between different unions, just as the pay varies between workers who are working in one industry as against another. The executive committee of a union determines the pay scales of their officials and, as the executive will be composed of members who are workmen in industry they will naturally want to make it worthwhile for the ordinary worker to leave his job to become a full-time officer. Therefore they will normally fix the local full-time officer's rate at a higher figure than the general earnings in the industry, and, of course, give him rights in respects of holidays and payment during sickness at standards not less favourable than the conditions which they themselves receive from their employers.

In short they will try to be model employers themselves, and do unto their employees as they would be done by.

When it comes to duties, the same general rule becomes impossible. A full-time officer does not expect a 48-hour week or a 40-hour week, or set hours of work. His job could not be done on that basis. He naturally expects to have to be available to service his members during normal day-time working hours but, in addition, he can expect to be called out to evening meetings and weekend conferences as part of his normal work. Obviously, if he has to spend nights away from home, and is therefore involved in extra expense for lodging or hotel accommodation, he should receive some recompense for that.

What most unions do is to lay down a scale to cover this, so that if the officer concerned has to address an evening meeting and has to buy a meal out, a modest payment, enough to cover the cost, can be claimed by him. Similarly in respect of overnight expenses, it is best to lay down a scale so that the official knows the limits within which he can move. These subsistence scales, of course, are more likely to apply to national officers and executive committee members than to local officials who normally will be able to get home each night from their evening meetings.

The cost of travel is also a cost which the union should bear: not the cost of travelling between home and office, if there is a separate office, but the cost of travelling from home or office to the meeting.

The number of branches to be helped by a full-time officer will naturally differ according to the size of the branches and their location. There is sometimes a difference of opinion about the size of a branch. A branch of 500–1,000 members can be administered at less expense and perhaps more efficiently than, say, ten branches or so with 50–100 members each. With a new and growing trade union, however, the system of smaller branches is generally preferable, for this gives a greater opportunity to a larger number of members to hold office in the union. In this way they develop their knowledge of union affairs in addition to developing individual and collective responsibility.

For example, each branch needs a chairman, a secretary, perhaps a financial secretary (or treasurer) and also a branch committee of five or six members. Every person who is elected to a position of this kind necessarily considers himself more involved and responsible because of his official status than he might be as an ordinary branch member. In the same way, the ordinary member of a small or medium-sized branch thinks, and sometimes rightly, that he has more opportunity of expressing his views and getting them accepted at a branch of 100 members, than he has in attending a branch at which there are perhaps 200 or 300 members present.

Yet another reason is that a small branch meeting lends itself to more practical discussion of union matters, and much less to demagogy. It is far easier for the demagogue to influence a gathering of 1,000 people with flowery or fiery language than it is for him to get 'steam up' in a small meeting place in front of perhaps 20 or 30 members. When vital and weighty decisions have to be made affecting the future of the union, it is calm consideration and reflection which is wanted, and that is more likely to be obtained in a score or so of smaller branches, for this gives every member the opportunity to ask questions, to put forward arguments, and to take part in discussion, so that, when the vote is finally called for, every aspect of the matter has been ventilated and weighed in each man's mind without passion or too much prejudice. The small branch, too, gives an opportunity for many members to air their opinion who would otherwise feel over-awed and reluctant to do so at a bigger gathering.

There is need in every union for all the abilities which human beings possess. There is need at times for the orator or the public speaker, and the ability to express oneself in this way, sometimes a natural gift but which more often has to be learned, is to be admired. The contribution to discussion, however, which earns a man the reputation of being 'a good man in committee' is also to be admired, and in trade union work particularly the qualities required are those of the committee man and the negotiator rather than the orator, whose strong field of activity is more often to be found in the political sphere. Sometimes it may be that the qualities of the orator, the committee man and the negotiator are to be found in one person, in which case that man can truly be regarded as 'thrice-blessed'.

The union branch meeting usually takes place every four weeks and is generally fixed for the same day of the month, such as the third Thursday or the second Wednesday, or whatever day seems to be most suitable for the majority of the members.

At the first formal meeting of a new branch it is usual to elect the officers and committee to serve for a year, and for them to be available for re-election at subsequent annual meetings. The branch secretary frequently continues to hold office for longer than a year without being re-nominated; it is often thought that the office of secretary is one in which continuity is most important, for although it is in the written records of the branch that decisions are noted, the circumstances surrounding the decisions are also important, and these are recorded in the memory of the people involved rather than in the minutes.

Good secretaries are more necessary and rare than good chairmen, for the secretary is more often the real leader and adviser of the branch. The reason for this is fairly obvious. It is the secretary who has the job of writing the minutes of the branch proceedings and this in itself tends to fix things more firmly in his memory: he deals with all the correspondence which passes between a member and the branch, between the branch and the local official, between the branch and the head office, between the branch and the local employer or employers, the local authority or the local office of different government departments. He learns to select that kind of correspondence which he can deal with as a matter of routine, reporting to the branch what he has done in their name, and getting their approval for it later.

In other cases of greater importance he will wait for the branch meeting and receive their instructions as to the kind of reply the members will want him to send.

Gradually the secretary becomes a walking encyclopaedia of knowledge about every facet of branch and union work: he knows the members well because he is more frequently in contact with them; he hears of their difficulties and problems because it is to him they will go for advice and information on every problem which crops up. The branch secretary is the man to go and ask, for the other members will say that 'if he doesn't know, he'll soon find out'.

In this finding-out process, the secretary becomes more and more expert—and indispensable. 'When you've got a good branch secretary, don't make him put up for re-election every year: it might give him the chance to stop doing that work' is a comment that is often made. Often the rules are worded so that after the branch secretary has been elected the first time he will 'continue in office as long as he continues to give satisfaction to the members'.

In addition to dealing with the correspondence and other matters, the branch secretary often deals with the collection of union contributions: he is helped in this work by the collecting stewards—that is, ordinary members of the branch who are willing to give a hand in collecting the weekly contribution from other members who perhaps do not trouble to attend the branch meetings but who are nevertheless interested in what is taking place.

A collecting steward may be responsible for collecting the subscriptions from 50 members or so at his place of work, or maybe ten members or even fewer. The collecting steward must be authorised by the branch to do this and, when authority is given, he can accept contributions from a member, enter up the amount he has received on the member's card—which is the member's receipt for the money—and then transmit that money, along with the other contributions he has collected, to the branch secretary.

The branch secretary enters into the branch register each member's contributions, so that he can see at a glance which members are paid up to date, which members are getting into arrears, which members are sick, unemployed or injured; as branch secretary he will probably arrange for them to be visited.

All this may sound as though the branch secretary has got to be a combination of clerk, accountant, teacher and lawyer and everything else. Actually that is not so. What the secretary needs is integrity and honesty, the ability to read and write, to do some simple arithmetic, to write down the money he has received, and where it came from, what he has spent for the branch and how he has spent it, and to show receipts to the auditor. The union's head office accounts may need to be handled by someone with a knowledge of book-keeping; the branch secretary is not expected to have that degree of skill.

The secretary, then, soon becomes the lynch-pin of the branch. 'A good secretary', it is sometimes said, 'makes a good branch.'

The job of the chairman, of course, is also important, but he functions mainly on the branch meeting night or on those occasions between branch meetings when the committee meets, usually once a month also. The branch members will expect their secretary to consult the chairman on any urgent action which may be required between meetings, and the chairman and the secretary then to act together on their behalf.

The main function of the chairman generally is to preside at the branch meetings, to see that the business is properly dealt with in accordance with the rules, and to ensure that the members have a full opportunity to express their views and elicit information about the decisions taken by the branch executive and about work undertaken by the secretary, and also to ensure that the various differing views which may be held by the members about any proposal are properly discussed.

49

The chairman, whatever his own private views, must be impartial: it is in the interest of the union and the members that opinions and views should be expressed one way or the other so that when the members are called upon to decide it cannot be said that any member who had some different viewpoint to express was excluded from the discussion. In a small branch meeting there can be less formality than in a bigger branch, but the chairman nevertheless must exercise exactly the same discretion and conduct the proceedings with the same sense of dignity as he would a larger meeting.

Sometimes the chairman has to protect 'the platform' (that is, the committee) from 'the floor' (the members generally) and also 'to protect the floor from the platform'. It is a position which calls for integrity and fairness, patience and understanding. A member with a minority view on many matters can easily develop into a branch malcontent, especially if he thinks he is being unfairly treated or suppressed by the chairman. The member may, in the opinion of everybody present, be talking nonsense, but it is the duty of a chairman to ensure a hearing for him as well as all the others. The chairman's authority will usually be the stronger the more lightly it is exercised.

A financial secretary or a branch treasurer has duties which are light compared with those of the branch secretary, and sometimes the latter combines the two posts. Where there is a separate financial secretary it is his job to deal with all the financial business of the branch, to make a monthly report to the members at the branch meeting about the state of the funds, to make sure that for every penny of union expenditure a receipt is obtained, and to give a receipt to every collecting steward for the money handed to him.

An annual audit of the branch accounts is usually considered satisfactory but a financial secretary may prefer to have an additional half-yearly audit; if some item has been overlooked it is easier to think back six months than twelve.

In Britain only a tiny fraction of branch secretaries are full-time officers, and they are the secretaries of a few giant branches, perhaps of 2,000–3,000 members. Most branches pay a token amount to their branch secretary as an appreciation of his work, and for a year's work this may be the equivalent of a week's wage or a little more. Whether it is more or less depends on the size of the branch.

Branch chairmen are never paid; a financial secretary may be given an honorarium which is about a quarter of that given to the branch secretary. The collecting stewards are paid about 10 per cent of what they collect and this may be paid to them at the end of the financial year or at the end of each six-month period. This, too, rarely adds up to more than the equivalent of a week's pay for the whole year although where a collector has, say, a hundred members on his books, his 'commission' may be the equivalent of two weeks' wages a year.

The agenda for the branch meeting, on which all reports are itemised, starts off with apologies for absence which are the explanations for non-attendance of some members—working over, sick, called away and so on. Next comes the reading of the record, the minutes of the last meeting. The chairman will ask whether they are approved as a correct record, and if that is agreed he signs them, and also puts the date under his signature.

The chairman then asks the secretary to report what action he has taken to carry out the decisions recorded in the minutes, and also invites any member to ask any question 'arising out of the minutes'.

The next item on the agenda will be the branch committee's report, and this will be given by the secretary. He tells the members what items the committee has considered since the branch's last meeting and the decisions they have made about them; he draws attention to certain items which have been passed along to the branch for decision. The chairman again invites questions, and a member who might want to disagree with one of the decisions which the committee has made may move the 'reference back' and explain why he is doing so.

The 'reference back' is what it says. He is asking the branch not to approve the committee's decision but to refer that item back to them to reconsider their decision. The chairman will ask if there is a seconder to the 'reference back', and if there is, the whole question is open for anyone to speak for or against the committee's recommendations. If there is no seconder there is no debate. If, however, the matter is debated it is up to the committee to convince the members that their recommendation is a wise one which should be supported, or for those in opposition to convince the members to the contrary.

When the chairman thinks everybody is quite clear on the issues involved, he takes the vote. He asks first for those in favour of the reference back to put up their hands, and then those against the reference back—that is, those in favour of the committee's recommendation. He then declares the reference back either carried or lost according to the voting, and the meeting goes on then to approve the committee's uncontested recommendations.

The next item on the agenda will be 'correspondence'. Any letters or communications of an informative character from the union head office will be dealt with first, then those from the district secretary, then any local correspondence from the members or employers or local organisations of any kind.

When all the correspondence is out of the way, the chairman will then ask for 'reports'. These will be the reports from members who represent the branch on any local committees, perhaps the local authority's Road Safety Committee or the technical education sub-committee or perhaps a report from a member who has attended a conference as a delegate on behalf of the branch.

The members are given the opportunity of asking any questions they wish on matters arising from these reports as they are given; at the end of each the chairman will ask if it is agreed that the report be 'received' or 'noted'. It will be 'noted' if that is the finality; 'received' if it is understood that the matter is still incomplete.

The last item on the agenda will be 'any other business' and this is the time when the chairman must really be on his toes for under this heading surprise items may be raised. A number of members may have had to leave the meeting, and this is just the time when some member with a particular desire to get a decision rushed through will be on his feet. If it is a comparatively simple and urgent matter, the chairman will let the member continue and allow a decision to be made. If it is a matter which the chairman thinks is so important that the branch as a whole should have advance notice of what is going to be raised, he will say that this seems to be a matter of which 'formal notice' should be given, and advise the member concerned to write out his motion in full so that the secretary can then put it on the agenda for the next meeting.

In this way the members of the branch will know what is to come before them and will be able to think about it before they attend the next branch meeting. They will be able to give a better-considered judgment and have a more representative vote, which is much wiser than having a decision on an important issue pushed through at the tail-end of the meeting on a 'snap' vote.

The chairman may have to be quite firm about his ruling, but it is his job to make sure that the rules of procedure are observed and also to protect the branch from being used to suit the convenience and wishes of a small group instead of the wishes of the members as a

53

whole. The chairman is the custodian of the branch's integrity; just as he must protect the member's rights, he must protect the rights of the branch, which is all the members collectively.

6

Wage Negotiations

A WAGES claim often starts off in a very simple and
homely way. It can start off with one member taking the
opportunity of speaking at the branch meeting under
the heading of 'any other business'.

At a branch meeting in Sheffield one of the union
members did just that. He started by saying that he had
had an argument with his wife who had given him only
a poached egg on toast for his Sunday dinner. Everyone
wondered what was coming next, and there were a lot
of smiling faces in the branch room. The chairman was
listening intently, not sure whether to ask what this had
to do with the branch or whether to let the speaker go
on. He was obviously not a very good speaker and did
not often have much to say.

The chairman was lenient and let him continue. A
poached egg on toast, the member said, was a very poor
substitute for roast beef, and so he had objected strongly.
His wife then had given him a list of about twenty
articles which had all gone up in price, and told him
that unless he gave her more money it would be only the
toast the next week, without the egg.

How could he give her more money, the man asked his
wife, when he already gave her all his wages? So she
told him he had better tell the union they ought to
get busy; wasn't this something he should raise at the
union meeting?

'So Mr Chairman, what about it?' asked the member.
'I like roast beef.'

The members, it is true, had quite a laugh about that,
but then others began to quote examples of rising prices,
and a big discussion was soon on its way. After a while

the chairman said this was too important a subject to be dealt with at the end of a meeting and he asked the members to agree to adjourn the discussion so that the committee, 'in the light of what had been said, could prepare a motion for circulation to members for a full discussion at the next meeting'.

At the committee meeting, facts and figures were mentioned by different members, one saying that, even on the basis of the Ministry's own cost-of-living index, there had been an increase of seven points since the last wage increase. The index was now at 132 as against 125 twelve months before. There was an argument then about whether that was 7 per cent, and the secretary explained that it was a seven *point* increase, not 7 per cent. He has worked it out to be 5½ per cent.

Yes, said somebody else, but the 5½ per cent was on the cost-of-living index as a whole. If the increases were calculated solely on the cost of food, it would be nearer to 10 per cent. He had collected information about prices of ordinary, everyday foodstuffs as they were just over twelve months ago and compared them with prices now.

Another member of the committee gave his opinion that in another three months the cost of living would have gone up again even more sharply; he thought they ought to recommend the branch to put in for a 15 per cent wage increase.

There was some head-shaking about this because three shillings in the pound was hardly likely to be a realistic claim. The majority seemed to think that if a claim was made for 7½ per cent—that is, eighteen pence in the pound—they would be more likely to get some sort of reasonable response from the management; nobody was in favour of the more cautious suggestion that the increase should be related exactly to the seven point increase in the index.

Eventually a motion was tabled and agreed: 'That this branch instructs the national executive to lodge an immediate claim to the employers' association for an increase of $7\frac{1}{2}$ per cent on the basic wage, bearing in mind, among other things, movement of the cost-of-living index since the date of the last wages settlement'.

There was similar argument at the branch meeting to that which had taken place at the branch committee, but finally the committee motion was approved and the secretary instructed to forward it to the district committee. The branch representative on the district committee was told by the branch that the motion must be 'spoken to' with emphasis when the district committee met. In addition, the secretary was instructed to ask the district secretary that the motion should be sent to all branches as a matter of urgency in advance of the district committee meeting.

Meanwhile the district secretary had received a similar motion from another branch, and he had no difficulty in agreeing to meet the request for an advance circular. At the district committee, a similar discussion took place, but the committee decided that, coupled with the request for a wages increase, there should also be a claim for the overtime rate to be increased, as this too had been the subject of repeated requests from branches. This overtime rate had been fixed at time-and-a-quarter for the first two hours, and time-and-a-half thereafter. The request now was for overtime to be at time-and-a-half instead of there being two different rates.

So off went the resolution to the national executive who had received two similar letters from other districts. The executive decided that they ought to have a special conference to consider these motions as well as their own recommendation. Their recommendation was that the union should ask for a 'substantial increase' instead of being tied down to a figure of $7\frac{1}{2}$ per cent or any other figure. They confirmed the overtime proposal in their recommendation and also a claim for a second week's annual holiday with pay, which had come from other district committees.

The general secretary duly summoned the conference; the executive's motion was sent to all branches with a request to them to discuss the motion and appoint delegates.

In some cases the branch instructed the delegate how he must vote at the conference. That is called 'mandating' him, or giving him 'a mandate'. In other cases, the branch left their delegate with a 'free hand'. That meant they were saying to him that as he had heard the discussion at the branch he should vote accordingly at the delegate conference unless he heard some argument there which has not been expressed at the branch. He was free, therefore, to cast his vote in the way he thought would be best in the interests of the members he was representing.

Actually, this latter method always seems to be the most sensible. If every branch delegate were to be mandated before he went to a conference there would seem to be no point in the conference itself, for the vote could be taken merely by asking each branch to send a postcard to the general secretary saying whether they were 'for' or 'against' a motion.

Of course, one of the main objects of the delegate conference is not only to ensure that the members are consulted through a democratic procedure but also to ensure that when the wage claim is submitted to the employers it will be known that this claim is not just a happy thought by a trade union leader 'keeping himself in business' but is the expressed decision of the members.

A conference, too, gives the leaders the opportunity of assessing the strength of their members' opinion in support of the claim. Are they simply saying 'yes' to the idea of a $7\frac{1}{2}$ per cent increase because everybody is always glad to have some extra money? Are they saying $7\frac{1}{2}$ per cent but really willing, perhaps, to settle for $2\frac{1}{2}$ per cent?

Or are they saying that they will fight strenuously to get the $7\frac{1}{2}$ per cent in the belief that this would be fully justified and anything less resented? All these 'feelings' will be crystallised at the conference, and that is undoubtedly its real value. It is a sounding board from which the leaders can assess the true feeling of all the branches.

The conference, too, by bringing the branch representatives together from all the districts of the union, lets the representatives see the link which brings them all together in the one union; the small branches in the weak, backward areas can see that they are not alone and isolated. Yet another advantage is that it gives an opportunity to the leaders generally to mix with the branch representatives, during the conference itself, at meal-breaks and socially, and so to be further informed, in a conversational way, of all the thought and developments taking place among the members.

Also, it is on the conference floor that the leaders of the future are to be seen and heard, speaking at the rostrum, challenging the platform when necessary, debating with other representatives. Such potential leaders are remembered, either favourably or unfavourably.

If the upshot of the conference is confirmation of the national executive's recommendations, usually moved by the general secretary, the first step of the general secretary, after the conference has dispersed and the executive have had a quick informal meeting to confirm the decision and discuss tactics, is to send a letter to the employers' association leader, often called the director, asking for a meeting.

This letter is not a memorandum or document setting out all the union's arguments. It is a brief, formal and courteous letter, asking for an early meeting to discuss a claim for a substantial increase in hourly rates of pay—because that was what the conference motion said—the question of overtime payment, and an extension of the holidays-with-pay agreement. The letter will go on to say that the main basis of the claim is on account of the increase in the cost of living, coupled, if this is the case, with greater output or improvement in the economic state of the industry.

The reply inevitably will be that the employers' representatives will be prepared to meet the union on a date convenient to both sides; and perhaps, expectedly, will say that the likelihood of being able to meet the union's claim is not great, that although there has been a small increase in output, the benefits of this have been offset by increased costs in other directions and that in fact profits over the period have not been high.

On receipt of this the general secretary gets in touch with the employers' representative, perhaps by telephone, to see what dates would be convenient to the employers, and each with their diaries in front of them they will fix perhaps two or three dates which could be mutually acceptable. Then will follow some quick telephone calls by each of them to their respective chairmen and committee members, followed by another consultation between themselves to compare notes.

This business of arranging dates can be very difficult, because all the people involved are busy men, all of them with commitments entered into a long time ahead and some of which it may be impossible to cancel or to re-arrange. Bearing this in mind, each side will be anticipating that it may be two or three weeks—a month perhaps—before the meeting can be held. The employers will be aware that there is pressure on the union leaders from the members to get a quick meeting, and that if the preparations become too prolonged there is danger of union members in the strongest branches deciding to take the matter into their own hands and call their members out on unofficial stoppages, which are helpful neither to workpeople—or employers—or the union's responsible leadership.

The meeting is eventually arranged, often at the employers' association office, and the discussions or negotiations start. The chairman and general secretary of the union, plus four or five members of the national executive will represent the union, and a similar number of employers, led by their chairman and director, will represent the employers' association. The size of this meeting varies, of course, but 12 to 20 people is about the maximum at such a consultation or 'negotiations'. The union chairman will introduce each member of his delegation, and the employers' chairman will do the same on his side.

Although it is a formal meeting, there will be some informality about it, too. The union chairman will very briefly thank the employers for receiving them and broadly state the reasons for the union's request—this should take about two minutes—and then ask the general secretary to state the union's case. When this has been done, the employers' chairman expresses his thanks to the union for their statement and usually asks that the employers should have an opportunity of considering the various points raised by the union, but meanwhile there are one or two questions they would like to ask to get further clarification.

The first question the employers are likely to ask is what is meant by 'substantial'? How much is 'substantial'? It could mean anything. At this stage the union general secretary will not commit himself to any figure, but will keep his statements vague and flexible. After several more questions, all of which will be dealt with by the general secretary (the other members of the union delegation leaving it entirely to him and contenting themselves with scribbling a note to him if they think there is some point he has missed) the employers' chairman will usually suggest that the meeting should adjourn for perhaps a week or two weeks when they will have had the chance to consider the union's statement and put forward a reply. A mutually convenient date is then arranged, and perhaps as the last piece of business and because the Press is waiting outside for a statement, the two sides agree that the director and the general secretary shall issue a short statement and that nobody else will discuss the matter with the Press.

Although the negotiations are private there will usually be a good deal of public interest, because other unions in other industries will be taking note of what the outcome of these negotiations is. Employers in other industries know too that whatever agreement is reached in these negotiations may be used as a basis for approaches to be made to them very shortly.

The Press statement will usually be only three lines or so, saying that the meeting was held, a claim was made, the meeting adjourned for the employers' association to consider it, and that a further meeting had been arranged for such and such a date. The employers' representatives, as well as those from the union, will want to let their members know what has transpired as a result of this first meeting, so the director will write to his member firms and the union general secretary will send out a circular letter to the union branches, giving little more detail at this stage than what has been said in the Press statement.

The members are thus 'kept in the picture' although it may only be to the extent that they know that something is moving.

In the meantime, if relations between the director and the general secretary are good and based on mutual respect, it would not be improper for the director to telephone the general secretary to ask him to clarify some particular point he has made and which the director thinks he may have misunderstood. If the general secretary is wise he will do this—and also report to his chairman about the clarification asked for.

At the next meeting the employers' representatives are ready to reply. The director, after the usual pleasantries about meeting again have been exchanged, will then reply to the union's claim. He will take up the various points made by the general secretary and give an assessment of the state of the industry and its prospects—usually not very rosy. At the conclusion of his case he may be able to say that because the cost of increasing the length of the paid holiday would mean an increase on production costs of about 2 per cent it would not be possible to concede this in addition to any substantial pay increase; however, he says, the employers generally were prepared, on account of the cost of living claim, to offer a 2½ per cent increase on the basic wage, but were not prepared to change the overtime rates.

The union general secretary, knowing the minds of his members and their expectations, will possibly reject this at once, without even consulting his colleagues who have also heard the director's reply. He will relate the employers' offer to what he himself had said in his presentation of the wages claim. He will take up the points made by the director, and then go on to argue for an increased offer from the employers, basing as many arguments as he can on the director's own statement.

This is now really the negotiating stage. From time to time other members of the union team, as well as the employers' team, will be throwing their ideas and arguments into the pool, although it is always preferable to leave the main statements to be made by the main spokesman from each side, the director and the general secretary.

When it becomes plain that the offer is completely unacceptable, the suggestion may be made by the employers that both sides should adjourn for half an hour or so, although this should not be regarded by the union team as being too hopeful a sign. It could be a black sign if the employers were to return and say that this was the maximum offer they could make. On the other hand, if they return with a slightly improved offer—perhaps a new offer of 3 or 3½ per cent, the union team may need to withdraw to consider this offer among themselves.

One or two members may want to reject the offer out of hand; somebody else will say they ought to go back and see if they can get it increased to 5 per cent. Another view will be that they will never get their members to accept 4 per cent, and they might as well give notice of termination of the agreement and start warning their members to stop work on a given date.

It may be suggested that if they could get the week's extra holiday as well as 4 per cent they could accept on that basis. Another suggestion, perhaps, is that they might ask for less than a week's extra holiday—say, three days—and the 4 per cent, and the extra overtime rate. Maybe they could settle on that?

This is a headache for everybody in the union team, for although they might be unanimous in rejecting the employers' offer, they might have seven or eight different ideas about the possible alternatives. They return to the meeting and tell the employers that the offer is still not acceptable; it is now for the general secretary to probe a bit further about holidays and overtime. From the discussion, some idea eventually emerges which looks a little promising, and again the two teams separate, with the employers returning this time agreeing to 4 per cent and the new overtime rate, providing that the union agrees to the abolition of some particular procedure which the employers have found irksome. Now the argument is directed towards this latest suggestion, and although it is contested fiercely, it begins to look as though some agreement can be reached.

It is open to the union to ask for an adjournment for a week if they wish, but if they think they can resolve the matter quickly, and carry their members with them, they will try for a quick settlement. They may ask for an adjournment so that they can come back with yet another idea. But it is obvious that the parties now are nearer together.

Eventually a settlement is agreed between them. It is now a matter for the union team to convince their membership that they have got the best settlement possible in all the circumstances, and this is the test of leadership. They know that there will be opposition to the settlement from some quarters but will the opposition be the majority or the minority? They know there will be few bouquets, but how many bricks will there be?

The leadership now is risking its judgment and maybe its future. If the leaders are timid and not prepared to make a strong case for what they believe to be a fair and just settlement, they will lose the day, and the result will be probably the election of new leaders with less sense of responsibility. This, too, would confront the employers with difficulties for it could lead to strikes which could be a disaster to the employers as well as the members of the union.

If the union leaders cannot honestly recommend their members to accept a proposed settlement they should not make such a recommendation. They are entitled to go to the members and explain what the final offer is and recommend its acceptance, or tell the members that no better settlement is likely to be reached without a strike. They must explain that after a strike it may not be possible to get even the terms offered now.

That puts the members in a quandary and they are entitled to ask what advice the leaders are offering. Since that is bound to the end-result, the leaders themselves must make a recommendation one way or the other at the outset. It is a big responsibility. It may be that a better offer could have been obtained, which would mean that perhaps thousands of workpeople are not getting as much in their pay packets each week thereafter as they should have. On the other hand, if the offer is in fact the best that the employers could make, and its non-acceptance is followed by an unsuccessful strike, the workpeople will have lost that much wages anyway.

There can also be a lot of difference between an offer before a strike, and the settlement which may ultimately have to be accepted after an unsuccessful strike.

Employers too have a lot at stake in these negotiations; they are involved, whether they like it or not, in the success or otherwise of the union's negotiators being able to get their members to accept the final offer.

If the employers' final offer is really the best they can afford, then even a strike will not bring a better settlement. If the union leaders have recommended the acceptance of the offer and their advice has been rejected in favour of action recommended from an irresponsible quarter, the union leaders' advice is likely to be accepted on a future occasion and the 'irresponsible' advice rejected.

On the other hand, if the employers have been holding out, or keeping something extra up their sleeve which ultimately they are forced to give as a result of a strike, then these employers may find themselves in future having to negotiate with people who will not believe the facts presented in negotiations, and who will submit demands on which negotiations will be impossible.

If a strike succeeds where ordinary collective bargaining negotiations fail it is certain that workpeople will remember this, with the result that the industry can become strike-prone with every claim being accompanied by strikes. If the leadership is being constantly changed as a result of every failure, it will be a long time before responsible leaders are able to emerge once more.

Therefore, honest, straightforward negotiating on the part of both sides is absolutely essential. Trickery or jiggery-pokery of any kind can only succeed once at the most, even if it succeeds at all; in return for that single act of dishonesty there will be years and years of bitterness, mistrust, suspicion and unnecessary obstinacy which will never be resolved until one side can lay a wreath on the other's grave.

Nor will skilful argument on its own win the day in negotiations. Persuasiveness based on facts, or reasonable conclusions drawn from facts, can help to put a favourable light on a claim. The intelligent approach of a practical man with a knowledge of the industry drawn from experience, or similar experience in another industry, is likely to convince the employers (who are also practical men in their industries) of the possibility of meeting the union's wishes.

It is this kind of approach which has become the traditional pattern of negotiations in Britain. Ultimatums, one way or the other, are never mentioned. What is the point of spelling out ultimatums when intelligent people know what they are without being told?

7

Conciliation and Arbitration

THE overwhelming majority of industrial difficulties are settled by negotiations which lead to agreement between the two parties. Nevertheless breakdowns in negotiations do occur, but even so nobody should be thinking in terms of strikes and lockouts because of that. In a strike, workers lose wages and incur debts for food and rent and other things which may take months to pay off. From a management viewpoint, if a factory is shut down it means no goods are being produced, contracts may be broken, orders may be lost, and profits are not being made.

So when wages talks break down the first thing to be looked at is whether it is possible to get talks going again quickly. In Britain at that stage it is open to either side to ask for the services of a conciliation officer, who is an employee of the Ministry of Labour, although work of conciliation could be done by anybody with ability who has the respect and goodwill of both parties and whose integrity is unchallenged.

The Minister of Labour, as a member of the Government, is necessarily a political figure; but the Ministry itself is not a political department. A conciliation officer is a civil servant and does not take sides, either politically or industrially. He is completely neutral as between employers and trade unions and he is available to an approach from either side without either side distrusting this move on the part of the other. Indeed, if a stoppage seems likely which will interfere with the public welfare generally, the conciliation officer might take the initiative and invite both sides to see him separately so that he may know what it is all about. As a result of these discussions, however they start, the conciliation officer may think he can see a glimmer of daylight through the problem; as he is a trusted man, he may be told, for his own information, something of the inner mind of the negotiators on either side.

Also he is an experienced man in this work, because in the course of time he will have had to deal with scores of conciliation cases, and is able to assess what the chances of a renewal of negotiations are and when to make the approach to get the talks started again. It is a delicate job, and his judgment about when the time is just ripe to step in may make a world of difference.

If negotiations are broken off and a week's notice is given of withdrawal of labour (or a month or whatever the period of notice may be) it is unlikely that the conciliation officer will start his interventions the following day. There is a week to go, and on the first two or three days each side will be flexing their muscles and both will be tight-lipped about the unreasonable attitude of the other side.

Nobody ever wants a strike, but nobody ever wants to be made to appear as though they are hoisting the white flag. It is when tempers have cooled down a little that the conciliation officer can be of maximum use. If his ear is close to the ground and if he is a good man at his job he will have met in the course of his work a number of people connected with both sides but not involved in the dispute who will be able to tell him what the real attitude is on both sides, which may be different from their public statements. Enthusiasm for a 'show-down' begins to evaporate a little the nearer one gets to it; both sides may be confident of victory, but each is beginning to weigh up the consequences and both are swiftly coming to the conclusion that a victory either way can mean a loss for everybody.

It is at this moment that the conciliation officer can make his most useful effort and get a response from the union and management. If he moves too soon he may be rebuffed by either or both: once he has been rebuffed the peace-maker is not too happy about risking the possibility of being rebuffed a second time. So timing is all important; this instinct or sixth sense comes from experience and from trying to imagine what normal negotiators must be thinking in these circumstances.

Only because he is completely neutral in these things can the conciliation officer make an approach. If he were not neutral, but thought by the employers to favour the viewpoint of trade unions, the employers would be reluctant to deal with him, and it would be the same on the part of trade unions if he was thought to be a 'management man'.

Armed with all the knowledge of the facts that he can collect, the conciliation officer will invite both sides to meet him, invariably separately at first, although his object is to get them to resume talks together and reach a settlement between themselves. It may not be long before he has got them to agree to have another look at the problem together under his informal chairmanship. If there is reasonable goodwill between the parties the obstacle which stood in the way of a settlement will soon be under examination once more. When there is enough goodwill between the two parties the new meeting can be arranged without the conciliation officer being present at all, but this is unlikely at this stage.

The conciliation officer's aim at all times is not to push himself into the picture but to be on hand in case he is wanted. If the parties seem as though they can reach agreement without his having to do anything else at all except push them into the same room, he is a happy man. He is not anxious for personal publicity; in fact he would rather run a mile to avoid it. It is a settlement he is after; somebody else can take the praise, if there is going to be any praise at all.

If a settlement is not reached as a result of this conciliation, the clouds are beginning to look very black indeed. Everybody outside the industry will begin to talk about arbitration; newspaper editorials will be written urging a settlement of the threatened strike by an arbitration board, by a judge, by someone.

The prospect of the two sides agreeing to an arbitration at this point is not too bright either, but the conciliation officer may not have finished his job yet. Although his first effort has failed, he will be on the telephone to both parties to see what can be done. He may consult the trade union national centre and the central employers' organisation to see if they have any helpful suggestions to make. He may ask one of the sides for further information about the main detail on which the conciliation proceedings broke down. If he can persuade one side that if they will depart, even a little, from the stand they have taken up to then, he will do his best with this small offering to see if the other side will come a little way to meet it. He will argue then that this creates a new situation and it ought to be examined.

The principle of give-and-take is the essence of all negotiations. Most trade unionists and managements know too much about life to expect 100 per cent from anything connected with human beings. There is no such thing as perfect people, and obviously then there is unlikely to be 100 per cent to be gained for either side in a settlement. For every 'take' there must be a 'give'; it is in this kind of situation that all negotiations are conducted. It is a question of balance. Is what one is getting worth what one is giving? That is the decision to be made. It is bargaining.

It may be that the two parties will agree to go to arbitration, though this is an infrequent decision if feelings on either side are running high. If an arbitration decision were likely at all the two sides would have agreed to let the problem go to arbitration a long time before the situation became, as it were, a great national and public issue.

Many agreements between unions and management specifically provide for their difficulties to go to arbitration; even where arbitration is not specifically written into the agreement, if relationships are reasonable any difficulty unresolved in the negotiations (and these will be few) may finally be dealt with by an arbitrator. Unions are often reluctant to declare in advance their willingness to go to arbitration because they think that arbitration may become the real aim of the employers rather than an attempt to reach a settlement by negotiations.

This is not because trade unionists think their negotiators may be out of work but because they want to have a say in the final settlement and believe that if every case were to go to arbitration it would begin to put too great a reliance on an authority outside the industry. They think that it should be possible for people on both sides who are conversant with an industry to settle their difficulties as equals at a negotiating table rather than being dependent on an outside authority like a professor or a judge whose knowledge of the industry may be small.

Union members usually would rather have their fate in their own hands than hand it over to a third party to decide what their wages or their working conditions or anything else should be. Also, if arbitration were thought to be automatic it might simply mean yet another stage of delay before a final settlement was made and put into operation. Arbitration can often mean delay.

Arbitration in Britain is rather different from many other countries. There are no High Court judges sitting as arbitrators, no counsel acting as they would in a great legal case in a civil court. Sometimes an employers' association may engage a QC to state their case for them at arbitration proceedings or at the industrial court. (It is not a court in the normal sense; there is no atmosphere of the law about it and its decisions are not legally binding although they are always accepted.) Trade

unions are always well advised to handle cases by themselves. It is only on matters of law that a QC or an
attorney has an advantage, and matters of law are not
relevant in industrial arbitration cases. It is the facts in
respect to a particular claim which count and a union
general secretary with his first-hand knowledge is much
better equipped than a lawyer to put his union's case
to the arbitrator.

On a matter which involves a union in normal legal
proceedings the union would be foolish not to get legal
advice, or not to be represented in court by a lawyer if
the occasion arose; but in courts of inquiry on industrial
matters, or when giving evidence before Royal Commissions, or on any other similar occasions, a general
secretary accustomed to negotiations and representation
will usually do a much better job than anyone else because he will have the facts of the matter at his finger
tips; the lawyer needs to work from his brief—that is,
present a case and argue it on the basis of what someone
else has told him. He has to deal with the matter second-
hand; that is a big handicap for him for a start.

Often enough the name of the arbitrator will be agreed
upon by the two parties, for an arbitrator who is not
acceptable to both sides could not succeed. Sometimes
the arbitrator will have sitting with him a representative
nominated by each side, whom he can consult, when he
is considering his award, about industrial technicalities
mentioned during the case. But it will be his decision
which will be given, the other two being advisers only.

On other occasions, when the arbitrator sits alone, he
will listen to the case made by both sides, ask questions
of both sides, and allow both sides to question one another to elucidate any point which may have come up
in the argument. When he thinks he has a clear picture
of the difficulty and both sides are satisfied that they
have told him everything he needs to know to make a

proper award, the proceedings will end, and his award will be sent to them later.

What sort of man is the arbitrator? He is often a man with a legal background, not because of his knowledge of law, because that is not involved in an arbitration case. His legal background is valuable because he is accustomed to weighing evidence, following an argument, and able to distinguish fact from rhetoric. He will not stop a representative from making the most flowery speeches; he is there to listen. But he will be more impressed with facts, quietly spoken and intended to give him all the evidence and facts on which the union has based its claim.

This type of presentation is usually most appreciated because the case then 'is speaking for itself'. A lot of oratory is sometimes used to hide or gloss over a bad case. The thin argument needs a big shout, but what is the use of a big shout if the arbitrator knows that, too? The arbitrator may be a professor, or an economist, or a retired civil servant, who has a knowledge of industrial practices, although not actually engaged in industry itself.

There are many such men, highly respected in their countries, who do this kind of work because they are interested or as their contribution to public service. They are not professional, that is they are not doing this job day-by-day or week-by-week and receiving a salary for it. There are not sufficient cases for that. An arbitrator whose name may be very well known throughout industry in Britain may get about £15 and modest expenses for listening to arguments from both sides, going home and sifting the arguments, and then writing his award. He is not likely to get rich in this way. In fact, such men are always rather proud of the fact that they are trusted to such an extent that both sides will call on them to settle a dispute. In a big industry an arbitration may involve an award of millions of pounds; the arbitrator's payment will be a few guineas.

Arbitration is a voluntary procedure in Britain; an arbitrator's awards, as has been said, are not legally binding. But as both sides have agreed to the arbitration the awards are morally binding, and that, of course, is stronger than law.

These things, then—negotiation, conciliation and arbitration—add up to what we call collective bargaining. In some countries there is another process called 'adjudication', but this usually means that the difficulty goes to a judge in a court and his decision is a legal one, binding in law. An appeal can be made against his judgment to a higher court; if either side do not like that result, the dispute can then go to the Supreme Court.

Cases dealt with like this have been known to drag on for twelve months and more; in the meantime there have been unofficial strikes, settlements by some employers with workpeople outside the normal collective bargaining machinery, and a general dissatisfaction with a procedure which turns the members away from trade union channels into political activity, for there are always people who are only too happy to take advantage of genuine grievances and transform them into action for their own political ends.

This kind of judicial machinery was designed for a different purpose from collective bargaining; it moves at a slower speed, and is not much use for industry. It is also doubtful whether this reliance on outside authority is helpful to the development of industrial democracy.

Democracy is not merely a matter of political method. It is a matter of social development. Anything which tends to take away from people collectively the authority of self-determination and replace it by the single authority of a person, whether a judge or a Minister, is encouraging a reliance on an outside authority and an enforced discipline. Democracies encourage collective authority and self-discipline; this is also the essence of trade unionism, and the essential and ultimate difference between democracy and totalitarianism.

Every endeavour should be made therefore to settle disputes by the collective bargaining procedure, and preferably at the negotiation stage without recourse to conciliation, and much less so to arbitration.

Strike talk, as a loose threat, is idle and mischievous talk; people who talk lightly about strikes are usually irresponsible. A strike or a lock-out is a final sanction, and the strike weapon is usually the stronger for not being used. A strong man rarely has to demonstrate his muscles; the wise strong man does not advertise his strength. It is only a foolish and weak man who is forever proclaiming how strong he is; at some point someone may call his bluff, and he cuts a sorry figure in the trial of strength.

There are many strong unions in Britain which have not had a strike for forty years or more. In the earlier days many had to strike for recognition but, having won that, their agreements, freely negotiated, ensure for their members a reasonable living standard and for the management an assurance of stability.

This outline of collective bargaining may seem to deal only with procedure where there is one union in one industry, but where there is more than one union the procedure is similar. Where there are two unions they should act jointly and this involves consultation and agreement between them before submitting their wages application to the employer. It is best for there to be some formal agreement between them about the procedure to be adopted so that no misunderstanding can arise, with one union going ahead on its own and accusations of bad faith, festering rivalry and bitterness developing as a consequence.

Where there are three or more unions concerned there *must* be a proper procedure agreement laid down so that everyone knows where he stands and what must be done to put the procedure in motion. The meetings with the employers in such cases will usually take the title of the 'Joint Industrial Council' or 'JIC' for whatever the industry concerned. This will be formal machinery, sometimes with equal representation from the unions and the employers, perhaps eight, nine or ten persons a side. Equality is not essential however for each side must agree as a side before decisions can be made. If there are three unions on the JIC with ten representatives between them, the division may be on the basis of six from one union, three from another and one from the union with the least membership in the industry; it is a kind of rough and ready proportional division of the seats.

The constitution of the JIC will provide for a chairman and a vice-chairman; often it will start on the basis of an employer being the chairman for one year and the vice-chairman a trade unionist, with the trade unionist becoming the chairman the following year and so on. There will be joint secretaries, one from the employers and one from the unions. It will probably be the union with the largest membership which will provide the secretary of the workers' side, who automatically becomes the joint secretary of the JIC.

Before the JIC meets, there will be a separate meeting of the union representatives to agree on their general proposals at the full meeting. At the full JIC meetings either side may ask for the discussions to be adjourned from time to time to give each side the opportunity of a private talk among themselves.

The basic principles of a JIC or Whitley Council proceedings involving a number of unions is little different from the collective bargaining procedure where only a single union is involved. Although on the JIC there may be representatives of craft unions, industrial unions and general unions, they function together on industrial organisation principles, while still adhering, as self-governing unions, to their own particular principle of organisation.

8

Economic Policy and Politics

MANY trade unionists in Britain support the Labour
Party and about half the unions in the TUC are affiliated to it. The Labour Party, however, has never at-
tempted to control the trade union movement or to
interfere in the domestic affairs of any union, either
affiliated to it or not. If any such attempt were made,
or to intervene in the affairs of the TUC, it would be
fiercely resented by all trade unionists and fought off.

A Labour government does not deal with the unions
and the TUC through channels any different from those
used by a Conservative government. Obviously the members of a Labour government are likely to have had more
and longer personal association with leading trade
unionists than members of other kinds of government
because they will have been present together on hundreds
of occasions at meetings, social functions, conferences and
so on. But trade unions do not trespass on this association, nor do Labour Party leaders think that trade unions
should have no contact or association with Conservative
Ministers.

Ministers are Ministers of the Crown, not of a Party.
A government represents the nation, not a political party.
It would be silly to boycott any government anyhow,
because trade unions, if they are to do their job properly
for their members, must be in touch with whatever
government is in power. Trade unionists claim the right
to make their representations direct to whatever government may be in authority, and consequently they must
accept the obligation to respond to government approaches for advice about proposals affecting industry
which are being contemplated. The policies of a govern-

ment may be distasteful to trade unionists but the political choice of the government is made by the democratic decision of the whole of the nation. Trade unionists recognise that although they represent an important and powerful part of the community it is in fact a part, whereas a government is chosen to represent the whole community.

The system of wage-fixing in Britain in general does not involve the government. The agreements reached are between employers and trade unions. Consequently, a change of government does not mean a change in the agreements which have been made within an industry. This continuing relationship in industry makes for stability and reduces the area of tension and excitement about the effects of changes which an election is bound to engender. Circumstances in which a change of government can take place without any dislocation of normal life should be encouraged, and since it is from industry and agriculture, trade and commerce, that a nation gets its wealth, trade unionism which continues to function on an even keel whatever political changes may be taking place should be encouraged at all points by everybody.

One is entitled to ask what is meant by stability in industry and good industrial relations.

In Britain, in the coalmining industry there are usually between 500–800 local strikes a year, mostly involving small numbers of people, and about 250,000 working days are lost. There are about 400,000 miners at work, so that makes an average loss of just over half-a-day's work for each miner out of, say, 250 working days a year. It means that instead of getting 100 per cent, we get 99·7 per cent.

In shipbuilding and ship repair, as in motor car manufacture, the percentage is also well over 99 per cent. In building the loss is usually less than two hours per man each year out of about 2,250 hours. Taking all employment together about five million days a year are lost because of strikes out of about 5,000 million working days, which means overall a loss of about three minutes per worker per week.

These figures are based on statistics from the Ministry of Labour Gazette, which is an official Government publication. The Ministry statistics cover official and unofficial strikes and also include the days lost by men who are not themselves on strike but who are deprived of work because of strikes. Industrial accidents cost Britain usually five times as much lost time as strikes, although safety at work is on a high standard; days lost because of sickness of one kind or another are about eighty times the number of days lost by strikes.

Any performance short of 100 per cent leaves room for improvement, but it is much easier to achieve 100 per cent accuracy if one is dealing with slide rules; dealing with human beings is rather a different matter and the margin of failure is bound to be greater. Nevertheless these official statistics indicate an achievement which can be fairly enough described as industrial stability.

Strikes, generally speaking, are bad news and consequently get headlines and big coverage, so that people often connect trade unions with strikes and little else. This is a fantastic impression because, in fact, without trade unions formulating with managements proper yard-sticks to satisfy both sides there could be local strikes on a scale which would bring chaos to a nation.

Most of the strikes which take place in Britain are 'local' and 'unofficial'—that is, they are undertaken by small groups of workpeople without getting in touch with the union first. There are usually about a thousand such stoppages a year, or half of the total stoppages, in coalmines.

Sometimes a difficulty at a factory may be in process of being sorted out between the management and the union but because a settlement has not been reached quickly the workpeople 'take the law into their own hands' and go out on strike against the union's advice.

Sometimes a strike blows up over some small incident, but the workpeople's resentment is so great that they walk out on the spot and only get in touch with the union at that point.

Unofficial strikes usually involve only a relatively small number of people and are usually of short duration. Some are about demarcation—that is, one group of workmen objecting to a workman of another trade being employed on work which is traditionally theirs. Some are about bonus payments, others about ventilation, or the dismissal of a workman, in the eyes of his fellow-workmen, unfairly. A stoppage can be about almost anything.

The reason for the actual stoppage sometimes appears to be small, but it is very often only the breaking point of long-time exasperation or irritants. Like an iceberg, it is not what one sees on top, but what is hidden underneath. What may cause a strike in one factory may be dealt with elsewhere in a proper, orderly way without difficulty. The difference, very often, since the problem may be the same in the two factories, is in the atmosphere of factory and workplace relationships.

The kind of industrial relationship which produces stability is as great a contribution to a reasonably high living standard as are up-to-date machinery and efficient organisation and administration in a factory. Increased production and better productivity depend as much on good industrial relations as on anything. Production, which is the source of a nation's wealth, is obviously the basis of social security for working people as well as the basis for good wages and reasonable working conditions.

In fact, everything which can be included in living standards, such as housing, health provisions, libraries, schools, street lighting and indeed all the services provided by local authorities and governments and paid for collectively through rates and taxes levied on individuals and companies, can only come from the products of industry. So good industrial relations are really at the root of both living standards and democratic development and modern civilisation. A union consequently is involved in the need to develop good productivity in the interests of its members.

A union is obviously concerned with safety standards at work and the elimination of industrial accidents, and joint committees in a factory or a works, composed of representatives of managements and elected employees, can be of enormous benefit to both management and workpeople. Sometimes managements seem reluctant to have joint committees, or if they accept the idea they seem reluctant to agree to the workpeople's representatives being limited to those who are members of unions. This is usually short-sighted because the workpeople who succeed in the election will mainly be trade union members since they are the organised workers; it is also better from a management view to have trade unionists on the joint committees because these workpeople will be able to get advice from the union about what is reasonable and unreasonable, for the union is also a centre of information about the different practices of other similar companies.

If workpeople only know what is happening in their own works they have no standards of comparison, and therefore no standard at all. They may, in fact, be asking for some things to be done which no management could meet, a kind of 'asking for the moon'. Workers are more likely to take cautionary advice from their union in such a case than they are from their own management.

In any case a management, if it recognises a union, has the right to go to the union for advice and assistance if the union members at the works are being unreasonable or obstructive. If the agreement with the union provides for a specified starting time and finishing time and a set meal-time, managements are entitled to exercise discipline on the basis of that agreement. Their hand is strengthened in dealing with recalcitrants by the fact that the agreement was made with the union, representing the workpeople, and the conditions were not simply laid down by the employers without consultation with anyone. Unions do not favour groups of their members breaking agreements any more than they like managements breaking them. A union can certainly co-operate with a management in operating an agreement, but it must not allow itself to become the instrument of the management. No management would wish a union to take over the management's functions, but sometimes, when difficult and distasteful tasks of discipline are involved, some managements try to push the union into making decisions which managements are paid to make.

The union always takes the view that full employment based on full order books and security are as important to its members as they are to managements and shareholders. It could be argued that these things are more important in their effects on union members than they are on shareholders, for if a worker loses his job with a firm he has lost the whole of his income until he finds another job, which may be difficult; if a shareholder loses a dividend from one firm it is unlikely that he has lost the whole of his income because most investors are unlikely to be 'carrying all their eggs in one basket'.

A method of joint consultation, too, provides the possibility for managements to inform workpeople, through their representatives, of industrial and mechanical changes which the management from time to time are proposing to introduce. There is nothing which causes more disquiet among workpeople than rumours about changes which management may be making, and trouble brewing over a long period can sometimes affect output to a greater extent than an actual short sharp stoppage.

Someone who hears half a story and has a lively imagination can supply the rest. Before very long the molehill has become a mountain; there is a saying that 'a lie can travel round the earth before truth can get its boots on'. Nor is there anything which irks people more than to learn news—either good or bad—at second or third hand when they reasonably could expect to learn it at first hand. The introduction of many good developments have been soured unnecessarily because information has 'leaked out' instead of being given out in a proper and recognised way.

The joint committee in a works is a proper and recognised channel for managements to discuss changes with workpeople, and this contributes to stability. One company which had big new orders had to introduce new machines to cope with the work and knew this would mean engaging more workpeople to run them. In less than six hours from the time the new machines arrived, and while they were still in their covers, the rumour had started that each of these new machines would do the work of ten men.

Someone who didn't want to be left out of the showing-off had 'actually' seen the list of people who were going to be sacked, and yet another knew also that this was so because he knew someone who knew someone else who had already typed the notice of dismissal to be given to workpeople either this Saturday or the Saturday after, he wasn't sure which.

What was true was that the new machines were better machines than the others, but that was the only truth in the whole rumour. (In time it was this new machinery that led to a reduction of hours and an increase in pay.) Meanwhile, however, the whole works was soon a seething cauldron of discontent and a strike lasting ten days was one result.

The other result was worse. The whole atmosphere of reasonable relationships was temporarily broken and it took many months before reassurance was again accepted. It takes years to establish confidence; it can be broken in a minute and always the process of re-building takes longer than before.

It can be said that sound trade unionism is as valuable to managements as it is to workpeople and the resultant relationship can be valuable to the nation as a whole. Industry functions better on the basis of good relationships.

Sometimes well-intentioned people think it would be better if other people stopped talking about the 'two sides' in industry. That is well-intentioned, but it is more realistic to think of the two sides working towards the same goal, recognising the merit of one another, understanding the rules and observing them. If this is done the idea of 'two sides' need not be deplored. The spectators will enjoy a good match, with no stoppages for foul play; the respect of the players for one another and the respect of the spectators for the quality of the play will also be good for the future.

9

Trade Unions and Production

'TIME and motion study' or 'work study' is a method used in industry, and offices too, to see to what extent improved production can be achieved while still using the same resources as before. 'Ergonomics' is a similar kind of study, the study of the workers' environment on the job, or studying the job to see how the workmen doing it can be helped by re-arrangement so there is less physical and mental strain for them. 'Cybernetics' is yet another study—of the way in which people's minds work in relation to the job they do. Sometimes all these are thought of together by workpeople under the blanket title of 'automation', and automation does involve consideration of all these things.

Trade unionists generally are likely to take the view that although no industry or factory can stand still while all the world is on the move, these developments should be viewed with caution. That is a reasonable reaction. If new developments and techniques are being introduced in industry they affect the livelihoods of individual workpeople, and it is the trade unions' job to protect their members.

But 'protection' does not mean stopping these developments, because that would be impossible anyway. All that could be done in that direction would be to delay the introduction of the new methods, but sooner or later, and sooner rather than later, it would be essential for the continuation of the industry that the new methods should be introduced.

Trade union leaders particularly, therefore, try to keep themselves informed of new techniques in industry, and so help their members to make arrangements to

87

develop the new process with as little dislocation as possible.

There are a number of ways in which the interests of the member can be safeguarded. If people believe there should be partnership in industry then the benefits of automation should give part-benefits to everybody. New and better methods should provide something extra as a return on the extra capital involved, because if people invest capital they do so on the expectation of some financial return.

Workpeople in the factory should benefit by better wages, shorter hours and longer holidays, if not at once at any rate on the basis of a promise, or an agreement or understanding, about these things. The community in general, who in the main are workpeople and many of them fellow-trade unionists, should also benefit on the basis of lower prices for the commodities produced.

All these things can accrue from automation, and indeed should. The production of more goods, that is, wealth, in shorter time should enable a higher living standard to be secured for the workpeople in the industry. There is also the possibility of a greater income for the Government from taxation which can be used to develop the social services necessary in a modern country.

New methods are never introduced overnight. That is an impossibility. Before new methods are brought into operation, they have to be thought about, and that thinking is obviously in the mind of management quite a time before they actually make a start.

After the thinking comes the tentative inquiries about the new machinery or methods. Even at the idea stage it is not too soon for management to start discussions with workpeople to explain to them what is in the managerial mind, how it is thought the new measures will apply, what it is hoped to achieve. If workpeople through their elected representatives are brought into the picture at this early stage, there will be less need for anxiety on the part of most, or for the fearful to stampede and panic.

Obviously management will be immediately interested in any possibility of developing new markets as a result of lower prices and bigger output, with consequently bigger commissions, salaries and emoluments. Work-people will approach changes more nervously for they may have more at stake. Will they lose their jobs? If unemployment develops, and if in the initial stages work-people are displaced, what is going to happen to them? Will they have to move their homes? If they do, what assistance will they be given? In short, what sort of guarantees can be given that their standards will not suffer, what sort of protection can they secure? They will be as enthusiastic as management about the hopeful results, but what if these hopes do not materialise? What then? It would be an odd workman who did not react along these lines and managements should expect to be asked these things.

In many cases managements will not be able to guarantee anything because until the change is under way they cannot know the positive results. All they really know is that their judgment tells them that certain results are likely. In other words, it becomes a question of judgment on the part of the management, and the question which arises is how much confidence the workers have in management's ability to judge.

The closer the relationship between them, the greater the mutual respect, and the greater the confidence. No management has the right to expect blind confidence on the part of the workpeople towards their judgments, and a responsible management will want to take work-people into their confidence to the fullest extent which is practicable. The use of the union representatives for this purpose will always be a reassuring thing, for these are the representatives who have been given the confidence of workpeople to look after their interests.

Redundancy or retrenchment, as it is sometimes called, can be a disastrous thing for a workman and his family, and any self-respecting workman will want to ensure the best arrangements possible at all times for his family, and secondly, for the well-being of his mates and fellow-workers. A workman who has no thought for their well-being is not likely to have much thought for his employer's.

The 'forward-thinking' of management and the responsible reactions of the union representatives will make it possible for large-scale changes to be 'phased' or spread over a period of time, during which steps can be taken to mitigate the worst possibilities, to blunt the sharp edges of the operation, and so avoid much unnecessary hardship.

Sometimes it is possible to arrange that for months before the new machines come in there will be no replacements for vacancies, and if someone quits his job for any reason the vacancy will be left unfilled and the work re-arranged so that the vacancy is covered by existing staff. This may mean overtime being worked by the others for a time—either at the usual rate or at a special rate negotiated by the union to meet this emergency—but this means one person less to be declared redundant if, in fact, any redundancy has to be declared.

Arrangements might be discussed as to the procedure to be adopted—and the principles—concerning redundancy. 'Last in, first out' is a widely-recognised practice which has the elements of rough justice and fairness. The local employment exchange can be notified, so that if they learn of vacancies elsewhere the first opportunity may be given to volunteers who leave this company.

It may be wise to assist with the removal expenses of workpeople who by their own endeavours have found other jobs; another assistance will be a gratuity related to years of service. Pensions may be introduced for some

of the older workers who have decided in the circumstances that they would like to finish work, and assistance
with payments for the re-training of other workers may
be useful.

Whether an industry is a nationalised industry or
private company, this kind of discussion and arrangement is necessary. With the development of technical
knowledge, new and wonderful machinery is being produced and used all over the world. It is often complicated
in structure though simple in operation. The more it
can do as an automatic process, the more expensive it is.
Very often it is too expensive for smaller firms to purchase, and the trend of the past will continue into the
future—that is, the smaller firm will need to merge or
amalgamate with other firms to make units or groups
with sufficient capital to purchase such machinery, and
sufficient scope for its use to justify the expense. In cases
where unions are based solely on one plant or firm, the
question of amalgamation or merger of the unions will
also arise.

In such cases there is a very strong argument for the
small individual union to look at its own organisational
problems in advance rather than to be overtaken by
events. A score or so separate small unions, each based
on a particular firm in an industry, cannot each provide
the services necessary for their members to deal with
problems created by this movement towards bigger units
in industry. Small unions should therefore be under-
taking an early move towards the formation, by amalgamation rather than federation, of national unions based
on the industry or the service or occupation for which
they cater.

One of the arguments sometimes used in favour of
nationalisation is that the capital and research required
in an industry for its maximum efficiency can only be
provided through national ownership; in general the
argument is that any industry which is essential to the

life and health and economy of a nation should be owned by the nation and developed in the national interest.

Many trade unionists think this is more likely to be undertaken properly if an industry is owned by the nation. The unions therefore recognise, indeed expect, that an industry can only be successfully run if it is efficiently run, and provided the latest scientific and technical methods are used towards that end. A nationalised industry which has a responsibility to the whole nation obviously accepts its responsibilities towards the workers in that industry, but if there should be a conflict between what is best for the workers in the industry and what is best for the nation, then the proven national interest must take first place.

The machinery for joint consultation which has been established in most nationalised industries is a powerful factor in ensuring that conflicts are kept to a minimum, and there is no doubt that if it did not exist there would have been many more clashes than have taken place. The idea that when an industry is nationalised this in itself means that the unions must accept all the decisions of management is shoddy thinking.

Trade unions take note of political changes and hope that governments which they support will create conditions in which the unions can carry out their industrial and economic duties with all managements as harmoniously as possible; but political events and decisions cannot themselves make economic circumstances change at every point. A government cannot guarantee a good cotton crop or sugar cane in abundance; nor, if there are such good crops, can they decide that other overseas nations must buy this produce, or themselves decide the price which manufacturers and dealers and users in other countries will pay. All they can do is to try to create favourable conditions for all these operations to be undertaken; 'banana spot' is not wiped out by changing a government although a different government may tackle that problem in a different way.

The only factor which remains stable is that wealth can only be produced by labour, and it can only be transported to the points where it can best be used as a result of people's work. Some work for wages, some for salaries, but whether it is hard physical work or worrying mental strain, whether it is manual or non-manual, operative, administrative or executive, industrial, commercial or clerical, the foundation of all wealth is work by someone or other.

The most effective work is organised work, and the most representative body for organised workers is a trade union. Trade unions represent that important part of the production of wealth, the workpeople: the other important factor is the management. If the quality of the work of management is poor, then the life of the nation suffers. This fundamental principle applies whether industries are nationalised or in private family ownership, or are public companies. Trade unionists get their livelihood, poor or otherwise depending on the success of the industry, from all three sources.

Members employed in any of these forms of industry have similar domestic problems to deal with. The worker who draws his wages from a nationalised industry spends them in the same shops as workers in other industries and pays the same price for a pair of shoes or a suit of clothes as the worker who draws his wages from Messrs X Y Z & Co Ltd or Henry Brown & Sons. So there is no discrimination by the unions for or against either kind of employment.

A trade union with members employed in the private sector and the nationalised sector must do its best for both: if it was thought by the union members that their interests were being sacrificed because their leaders favoured a particular method of industry-ownership it would not be long before that union either got new

93

leaders, found 'civil war' among its members, or, worse still, had to face the formation of a breakaway union by those members who thought they were getting a raw deal because of this partisan attitude of their leaders.

Efficiency in industry is bound to give workpeople a better chance of a higher standard of living than would be the case if the industry was inefficient. Sometimes workpeople may argue that increased production means unemployment and a lower living standard. The contrary would be that lower production means increased employment and a higher living standard, and that is absurd. Fewer clothes to wear, less food to eat, fewer shoes, fewer hospitals and schools, less unemployment benefit and lower pensions can only add up to one thing —a lower living standard. No trade union can ever achieve its fundamental purpose of improving living standards on that basis.

Modern trade unions therefore seek not only to increase production and productivity but at the same time seek to ensure that there are benefits for the community by way of lower prices, for workpeople by better wages and working conditions, and to ensure that profits are not allocated a disproportionate share of the surplus.

10

Trade Union Leadership

MUCH is expected of a trade union leader by the member-ship. That is natural. But much is expected of him, too, by managements and the general public. He receives a great deal of free and unsolicited advice from many quarters.

A trade union leader is responsible first and foremost to the members of his own union. He must carry out the policies which they decide at their conferences, or through whatever procedure policy is decided. He must give effect to decisions made on behalf of the members by the executive committee.

Before these policy matters are determined and any other decisions made, a leader has a most important job to do. That job is to get as much information as possible about the matter the members are considering, from all the sources he can think of, so that they may be fully advised. The leader has to advise and guide his members in their discussions. So he must first make up his own mind on the basis of the facts. In the course of advising his members he must put all the facts and arguments squarely before them so that they may have as much in-formation as he has. If he is interpreting the mind of his members correctly, he will know that the majority, in normal circumstances, will come to the same con-clusion as himself.

In some cases it may not matter very much what de-cision is made, but on matters of fundamental importance a leader must have something to say; he is expected to show his leadership and to carry his members with him in support. Whether the view he is going to put is popular or unpopular, whether he is going to be cheered or heckled—and in controversial matters it is usually a combination of the two—he must express his view and express it strongly. The leader who speaks his mind fearlessly in the interests of his members will be respected by them, even when his advice is rejected, which will be rare.

There is no shame on a trade union leader who loses the vote in a debate. There is shame on a leader who keeps silent because he is afraid of losing popularity. Even if he does lose on the vote, later events may well prove that he was right after all, and this will strengthen his position the next time.

A trade union leader must always be equipping himself for his leadership; he must spend much of any spare time he has reading official reports, keeping up to date about developments in his union's industry, keeping in touch with the members not only at branch meetings from time to time but also by being present at their social events. He has to be available to serve the union at all times, and everything else must take second place to the urgent needs of his members.

He must be ahead of his members in his thinking about their problems. It is his job to anticipate not only what happens next but what can happen after that and to be ready to meet whatever situations may arise.

Sometimes events move in the leader's favour, but inevitably they will move against him at some time or another. The wise leader always remembers there is always another battle to be fought which he may lose. So he doesn't crow about victories or gloat over his opponent in defeat. There is another day tomorrow and the cards may be stacked the other way round. Nor does he descend into gloom when it is his opponents' lucky day. He must be philosophical in all these things.

Whatever happens he must keep his integrity intact, for if he loses that he loses the respect both of his members and the employers with whom he negotiates. The temptation to win the day by debating tricks must be avoided for usually the people with whom he is negotiating are not naïve or innocent or inexperienced. They are experienced and practical men, and although it is not impossible that such men may be duped once they are not likely to be caught out twice. A reputation for honest dealing has to be built up, and then protected at all times.

If the leader does not earn and keep a reputation for honest negotiating and firm settlements he will not be able to get the best agreements for his members. He can be as tough as he likes, but when he has finally given his word there must be no turning back, no attempt to wriggle out of it because his members may be critical. He may have to use all his powers of persuasion to get his members to approve the settlement that he and his executive committee have made in the members' name: he can only do that if he believes that he has made as good a settlement as anybody else could have got in the circumstances.

It is his job, too, to advise his members realistically, and to refrain from making flamboyant speeches inciting unrealistic claims. Any fool can incite workers to go out on strike but it needs thought and brains to get improvements without a strike.

If the union negotiators can get a higher living standard for their members on the basis of stability within the industry, that is good for the members and their families, and for the employer too, for it helps him with his forward planning if he can rely on there being no dislocation in his works through strikes or labour disputes. After all, human beings are unpredictable in their reactions, and there is no algebra or trigonometry or chemical formula by which their emotions and actions can be mathematically worked out. The accountants and the statisticians in the works office can plot everything on a graph except the reactions of workpeople.

If there is stability in industry it is good for the nation, too, so that a trade union leader has another responsibility there.

Integrity and courage, thought and judgment, dedication and loyalty—these are all ingredients in the make-up of a successful and respected trade union leader. Stamina is required as well, for, oddly as some people think, there are no trade union rates of pay or hours or conditions for those who are chosen by their fellow-members to serve in trade union leadership.

The ability of a trade union leader to express himself well is something which can be learned. Speaking in public is not a matter of getting up on one's feet at a meeting and bombarding the audience with words. Different kinds of meetings call for a different approach. A piece of oratory at a great celebration—a union anniversary, a May Day meeting or a big organising rally in the open air—would not be very suitable at, say, a tribunal hearing of a wages claim, or to a small audience in a lecture room.

The first thing one has to do is to get used to the sound of one's own voice. Reading aloud in private is a good start, followed by some private practice in front of a mirror, which lets a person see himself in action as the audience will see him. In a great gathering or in a small hall, if the man in the back row is hearing everything clearly the man in the front row is bound to be hearing also. It is not necessary to bellow, but it is necessary to pitch the voice higher, sometimes a good deal higher, than in ordinary conversation unless, of course, one is speaking into a microphone. Even then it is important to let the words come out a bit more deliberately so that each word hits home clearly.

Gestures of emphasis with the hands should be made distinctly, and at shoulder-level. The audience is watching the speaker's face as he talks, and they will be able to take in the gestures at the same time. Slovenly dress or slovenly habits are no compliment to an audience; to many people these will give the impression of a slovenly mind or a lackadaisical, apathetic approach.

A lively speaker will usually be more attractive to an audience than one who looks as though he has just got up from a sick bed—so long as he does not throw himself off the platform. On the other hand, a lecture to a small group should be conversational while the presentation of a case to a tribunal should be rather more formal.

Usually, however, the harder part is not the presentation of the speech but the preparation of it. Preparing a speech is rather a different matter from writing an article. An article which is to be published can be read and re-read, so it may not be necessary to drive the point home more than once.

So the written word should be

> Hard as a stone
> Clear as a stream
> Clean as a bone
> Two words are not so good as one.

With either a speech or an article, the basic approach is the same. Think of the subject, think of the kind of audience to whom the message is going. Let the subject turn over in one's mind. Jot down on separate small sheets of paper the thoughts and the phrases as they come. Illustrations, similes, contrasts, arguments for and against, the facts one is sure about, the doubtful points, sources of reference which occur. Keep thinking and jotting: let one's mind travel round the subject at odd times during the day—on a bus, in a train, over a meal—but always keep the jotting pad handy.

The next step is to sort out the pieces of notepaper into some sort of order and, when the related points of the argument are brought together, to start expanding and developing each point. A busy trade union official has no time to write down every word of a speech. If he did that he would need a week to write a speech which would last about forty minutes. A forty-minutes speech means 5,000 words and to write all that takes time.

Once the expanded notes have been brought together in some sort of order, transfer the key words of each point on to postcards, printed big enough to be able to see the phrase at a glance so that the flow of the speech is not interrupted, which will mean that the flow of the thought in the minds of the listeners will not be interrupted either.

Assume that the audience is reasonable, open to persuasion; never convey that one is anticipating opposition even if that is the fact. Be courteous, even when hitting hard. Do not put on an act; it is easier, anyway, to be natural.

The first two or three minutes of the speech should be an opportunity for the listeners to get accustomed to the voice and perhaps the accent. During this time the audience will be observing the speaker and settling down after the chairman's introduction. These three minutes are really throw-away time.

Start the main theme of the speech by first outlining the problem; second, state the facts; third, set out the arguments for or against, illustrating and leading towards the aspect which the speaker thinks is the right view to take. Fourth, summarise and pull the facts together. Fifth, in the final four or five minutes finish off the case as a whole, persuasively and emphatically, with confidence.

A speaker who waffles towards the end can be in trouble. If he finishes up with an apology such as, 'Well, there it is. I'm afraid I've taken up a lot of your time but...." it only needs one wit in the audience to shout, 'We can all agree on that' for a roar of laughter to produce an anti-climax. If that happens, the speaker might well have stayed at home.

11

Trade Union Finance

BEFORE 1799, trade unions in Britain were outlawed in some districts and trades but tolerated in others. From 1799 to 1824 the unions were illegal and trade unionists were all 'illegal men'.

Some of the unions, though, were able to continue their existence in secret because the enforcement of law generally in those days was not so efficient as it is now. Being illegal, they could not put their funds in a bank but they did not trust the banks anyway. So most of the unions placed their funds in the safe custody of the landlord of the inn where they held their weekly meetings.

The rules of the London Society of Brushmakers, whose members met at the 'Craven Head' in Drury Lane, stated in 1806 'that a box with three different locks and keys shall be provided, each steward to keep a key and the landlord of the meeting house the other'. The two union stewards were what would be called today 'the trustees'.

By 1831 the Brushmakers had got together £400; it was all in the box, a huge brass-bound affair screwed down and stapled to the floor. This £400 was a lot of money. It could be a temptation to thieves. The members' minds also turned to the question of some interest on the money. They did not invest it in the name of the union because the union's rules laid it down that in any financial transaction the trustees and union officer must never mention their connection with the union. The union was 'illegal' and they were afraid of their funds being confiscated by the law on some pretext or another. The money was invested therefore in small sums with a very respected and wealthy farmer-brewer, each investment being in the joint names of two members.

Even in 1861, when the union decided that it could trust the new Post Office Savings Bank, the deposits were made in joint accounts by members 'who must not own their connection with the Union'. Fears of being outlawed still remained after so many years, and if that were to happen these funds might be confiscated if they were invested in the union's name. 'Funds', the Society said 'shall in future be invested in the Post Office Savings Bank, the sums not exceeding £30, in two members' names. . . .'

The total assets of the trade union movement in Britain are now over £120 million. All the bigger unions own outright their own head office buildings and district offices. Some of them also own house property because the pioneers always thought highly of 'putting their money into bricks and mortar'. They regarded that as being a very stable and solid investment and indeed so it turned out to be.

Most of these accumulated funds today are locked away in ten and twenty year loans in Government securities and municipal loans, bringing in an annual income virtually the whole of which in each union is used for the sickness, unemployment, accident and old-age benefit funds. Dealing with sums of this kind means naturally that firms of accountants now audit the books, and advise the unions on the complications of income tax and how to invest some of their money in industrial equities.

Before the unions reached this stage, the auditors were ordinary members of the union who were known to have 'a good head for figures'. Some unions, in order to try to avoid their funds losing purchasing power over the years, have started to invest a portion of their assets in companies, but as yet this is only a very small number of unions, and even in their cases only a very small proportion of their funds.

The emphasis in union investment policy is on keeping enough funds reasonably accessible to meet any unexpected circumstances which the union may have to face, and to invest the balance in such a way that the union knows exactly what the investments will be worth in the future. If a union's total assets were £10,000 and all of this was locked away for, say, ten years, the union would lose a lot of the value of these investments if they needed to cash them to meet an emergency such as strike pay or a lot of claims for unemployment benefit.

In the 1920s and '30s, because there was high unemployment (in such circumstances strikes are always more prevalent which may seem paradoxical but will be fully understood by industrialists and trade unionists) the unions needed to have a lot of 'liquid assets'—that is, cash, available to pay unemployment benefit and strike pay. The proportion of their total assets which was kept at the banks in cash was as high as one-third: only about one-half of their funds was in loans to governments and municipalities, and the remainder was represented by their buildings and property of one kind and another. An accountant would say this was a high liquidity ratio. In Britain now, with little unemployment and far better industrial relations, and with funds which have grown considerably, about four-fifths of the funds are invested in Government and municipal stocks, and only about one-tenth is in the form of cash in the banks.

Working people all over the world earn their wages in a hard way, and as a result their small savings are invested in the safest possible fashion. Consequently, when working people as active trade unionists have the responsibility for making decisions about the investment of the union's funds they are not likely to take a different view about how they should safeguard the union's money from how they would safeguard their own. In fact, since they are responsible for the funds which belong to the members, they are likely to be even more cautious with the investment of them than perhaps they might be with money which was their own individual property.

If a union executive is in any doubt it should get the advice of a bank manager or a professional auditor and accountant. The bank manager's advice will be free, as part of the bank's service; the professional auditor may charge a small fee for auditing the union's accounts and giving general advice, but this will be money well spent; as an expert he will be worthy of his hire.

There is always something to learn, and the pool of knowledge which is developed by union leaders discussing with one another these practical matters about funds soon becomes a reservoir of facts and experience which can be used more and more for the benefit of the trade union movement generally.

Trade unions are not businesses or companies and are not run on the basis of cold-blooded accountancy. If trade unionists were to go into every problem which comes up with a ready-reckoner in front of them instead of trade union principles being foremost in their minds there would never be a trade union movement. Trade unionism means brotherhood, and true brotherhood involves faith and confidence in one another. A trade union's concern is not so much with percentages and balances and surpluses as it is with principles of justice and fair play and square dealing, the principle of 'one for all, and all for one'. Nevertheless, as bodies of practical people, trade unions must carry out their functions in a practical way.

A union's strength is not in the thousands of pounds or millions sterling they can build up over the years. That may be true of banks and insurance companies and building societies and similar bodies. The real strength of trade unions is in the size of their membership in relation to the number of workers in the industry or trade or occupation for which they cater, in the loyalty and responsibility of the individual member. These items cannot figure in a balance sheet as a cash reserve but they are the union's real assets all the same. From a financial point of view, the capacity of the members to replenish trade union coffers for causes in which they believe or for purposes which they think are necessary, at the moment they realise it has got to be done, is an enormous reserve which can never appear in a balance sheet. It cannot be invested but it does exist.

The Trades Union Congress in Britain, formed in 1868, has only had a building of its own since 1956. The building—Congress House—cost over £1 million. The TUC had no funds to pay that or anything like that amount. But the unions felt it was about time there was such a headquarters and decided to contribute to a special fund tenpence extra per member for three years. There are over eight million members who make up the TUC, so that meant the whole cost was met in a very speedy way.

Similarly, the TUC contribution of £500,000 to the first International Solidarity Fund of the International Confederation of Free Trade Unions (totalling £2 million) was met quickly by a special contribution from the affiliated unions.

Although that sounds easy, an important factor must be kept in mind. This kind of special appeal cannot be made frequently, otherwise it ceases to be 'special'; and if it ceases to be 'special' and becomes the normal all-the-year-round-and-every-year practice, the members are not likely to respond with the same generosity or enthusiasm as they do for a special purpose to which they give their full support.

There are many proverbs about this sort of thing, about going to the well too often, about the goose that lays the golden egg, about overworking the willing horse. Some of these proverbs are as true today as when they were first spoken centuries ago.

12

National Environments

TRADE union movements in most countries have the same basic function, that is of trying to maintain and improve the living standards of their members. A country's historical background, its climate, its size and natural resources, are only some of the factors which affect the outlook and attitude of a nation. If food is growing on every tree and in every field, and the sun and the rain and the breezes are gentle in turn, the outlook of the people of such a paradise will be different from that of people whose lives are based on shortages and hardship.

The outlook and attitude of these people individually will inevitably express itself in the organisations which they establish collectively; so although trade unions, wherever they are free to do so, will develop the same basic philosophy towards life and labour, they will organise themselves in a manner most suitable to themselves in the light of their own background, knowledge, experience and necessity.

The structure of trade unions cannot be transplanted exactly from one country to another. The basic principles of democratic trade unionism, and some of its methods, are the same all over the world. A trade union however does not operate on its own in a vacuum. It works in association with other bodies, employers' associations, community bodies, town councils and Parliaments. It operates within national habits and popular conventions, and is itself constantly changing in relation to the social and economic changes taking place around it. In fact, the activities of a trade union itself help to bring about such changes; that is one of the union's intentions and objects.

The form, shape and attitude of a trade union, then, are matters conditioned by national circumstances at particular periods of that nation's development, and a trade union movement which tries to ignore these matters will merely become a group of theorists destined to play only little part in the growth of a nation and its people. It will be unrepresentative because it will not be working within the limits of reality and practicability. That is why a trade union movement must know its immediate objective, and be able to state that objective as a step towards a specific longer-term objective.

For example, in a country where a 48-hour week is the practice now it would be right for a union to declare its aim as being a 40-hour week, but it would know that to get there in one step would be unlikely. At such a stage to express aims beyond the point of a 40-hour week, except in the broadest and most general terms, would be unreal because the intervening period between the present time and the achievement of their 40-hour week aim might have seen such social and economic changes that it would make nonsense of anything stated so specifically.

A trade union is a pragmatic body, doing what it can, when it can and how it can, within the boundaries of the society in which it has its existence. Within the International Confederation of Free Trade Unions there are over 47 million trade unionists from 120 organisations in 94 countries. Not one of them is a carbon copy of another, because not one country is an exact copy of another. The Communist-dominated World Federation of Trade Unions is not allowed by Soviet Russia to recognise this important fact; as a result its only affiliates are drawn solely from bodies which carry out policies which are determined by the Communist Party in their own countries which, in turn, act under the direction of the Soviet Communist Party.

Each of the movements affiliated to the ICFTU, however, is completely self-governing, and indeed that is a condition of affiliation. Thus the Trade Union Movement of Israel has a different structure and methods from those of Sweden; India's trade union movement is different in its operation from that of its near neighbour Pakistan. The Malaysian TUC is different, too, from that of Singapore or Hong Kong.

It is natural that Britain's TUC should have played an important part in the affairs of international trade unionism and will continue to do so. It was in Britain that organised trade unionism first developed, and it was towards Britain that young and growing trade unions looked for their advice and inspiration. That is still true today, and many national trade union centres look directly towards the TUC for information and guidance, although this does not lessen their or the TUC's activity within the ICFTU or diminish their loyalty to it.

The International Labour Organisation, which has its headquarters in Geneva, is a governmental agency, supported and financed by 121 governments. This has a different operation and function altogether from that of the ICFTU. Representatives of governments, advised by representatives of trade unions and employers' organisations in each country, meet to lay down international minimum standards in social security, industrial safety and welfare, and to outline conditions of work and the kind of action governments should take to improve living conditions in their own countries.

Trade union movements in the Commonwealth have strong links with the TUC, as might be expected. All of them are independent, self-governing trade union movements and they would laugh at any suggestion that they are controlled from London by the TUC. Like all other national trade union centres, the trade union movements of the Commonwealth are equal partners in the great international association of trade unionists, ready to give a hand to every other democratic trade union movement; they have no hesitation or embarrassment, when in difficulty, in asking for assistance, advice, information or guidance. In this way they have often been able to avoid the pitfalls and difficulties about which others have had to learn by painful experience.

13

Outline of Different
Trade Union Movements

In Britain there are 54 million people on a very small compact but highly industrialised island, with hardly any natural resources or raw materials. Most of Britain's food has to be imported, and also most of the raw material for industry, except coal and iron ore. The country has a long historical background in industry, commerce and social development.

The United States of America is comparatively young with a population of over 200 million people, spread over a vast continent which is rich in agricultural production, raw materials and natural resources such as great rivers which can be harnessed for electricity supply. Its population has been largely immigrant.

The Soviet Union, too, is a big continent, with a population of 240 millions and great natural resources, plus vast supplies of raw materials. Industrially it is a young country also. Historically, Russia is old.

Here then are three countries with some similarities and enormous differences. Their trade union movements also reflect these differences and also some similarities.

The situation of the workers and of the trade unions in the Soviet Union are very different from those which are found in most other countries; the structure, functions and rights of the Soviet trade unions cannot properly be understood unless one understands also the economic, political and social structure of the Soviet state. Private ownership of the means of production has been abolished in the Soviet Union but this does not mean that social distinctions and privilege have been abolished. In fact, new distinctions and social inequalities have developed meanwhile. What it does mean is simply that because of this fundamental change in the ownership of the means of production the place of the worker has changed radically, because these means have become technically the property of the people.

There are no longer any private employers in factories and farms, but industry and agriculture nevertheless need labour and the workers need employment. Their work must be arranged and supervised, arrangements for paying the workers must be made, the average amount of work expected from workers in a factory must be set, i.e. 'norms' must be established; the working conditions, hours of labour and paid holidays, starting times, finishing times and all the other items normally covered by collective bargaining must be set. In democratic countries, this is mainly done by collective bargaining between independent unions representing the workers and controlled by them on the one hand and the management on the other.

In the Soviet Union neither the management nor the unions is independent; since both are controlled by the Soviet Communist Party which also controls the Government, to which no opposition Party is allowed, it is difficult indeed, after the common use of the term 'trade union', to find common ground of comparison with other trade union movements.

The Soviet Government has passed along to the Soviet trade unions the responsibility for supervising a national health service and also a national insurance system for the payment of sickness benefit, old-age pensions and so on. It has also arranged that State funds shall be available to the Soviet trade unions for that purpose. The placing of people in jobs is another function which the State has passed along to the trade unions. Arrangements for workpeople's housing are made through the trade unions, which also arranges for creches and kindergartens to be maintained and staffed at factories. Holiday resort accommodation is arranged through trade union channels also. In many respects, the Soviet trade unions perform functions which in other countries are carried out by a number of different government departments, such as a Ministry of Labour or the Ministries of Health, National Insurance and Education.

The preamble to the rules of the Trade Unions of the USSR, adopted in March 1959, contains the passage:

'The Soviet trade unions, which are a mass, non-party public organisation, unite on a voluntary basis, workers and other employees of all occupations, irrespective of race, nationality, sex or religious beliefs. The Soviet trade unions conduct all their activities under the guidance of the Communist Party of the Soviet Union, the organising and directing force of Soviet society. The trade unions of the USSR rally the masses of workers and other employees around the Party and mobilise them for the struggle to build a communist society.'

Another statement, still included in the preamble to the rules of the Trade Unions of the USSR, was that put forward by Lenin in 1921; it is that the trade unions must remain 'an educational organisation, an enlisting and training organisation . . . a school, a school of administration, a school of management, a school of Communism'. In this kind of relationship, it seems evident that there could never be any final disagreement between a management and a trade union and the Government since all three are the same, but wearing a different hat. Any disagreement on the part of the workpeople over a settlement reached about the rate for the job or working conditions which expressed itself in an unofficial stoppage of work—and there could never be, under this arrangement, an official stoppage of work—would be judged an offence against Article 6 of an Act adopted on December 25, 1958, concerning criminal responsibility in offences against the State. This says:

'An act of commission or omission aimed at undermining industry, transport, agriculture, the monetary system, trade or some other branch of the national economy, or the activity of a State agency or public organisation for the purpose of weakening the Soviet State, if such act is committed by utilising a State or public institution, enterprise or organisation or by hindering its normal work is punished by deprivation of freedom for a period of eight to fifteen years and confiscation of property.'

On the other hand, for what it is worth, strikes are not specifically prohibited by law in the Soviet Union. The usual reply given to questions about strikes in the USSR is that in any case the workers do not have to resort to strike action as there is nobody for them to strike against since the means of production belong to them.

In many other countries in the world there are great industries which belong to the nation. A similar reply given in those countries might sound a little odd.

The Soviet trade unions are usually organised on industrial principles—that is, one union for all workers and employees in one industry, although the designation of the industry varies from time to time. In 1941, there were 192 unions, in 1949, 67 unions. These had been reduced to 43 unions in 1954 and to 22 in 1959 with a membership of 52.78 million. This fluctuation in the number of unions is mainly to adapt trade union structure to changes made in the economic and political administration.

In November 1962 sweeping changes were imposed on the Soviet trade unions by the Soviet Communist Party central committee. These changes split the unions in two, at regional and local levels, to follow the re-organisation of the Communist Party itself and the parallel re-organisation of the local and regional Soviets (municipal councils). One section of the new split trade unions will concentrate on agriculture and the other on industrial production. The object is to concentrate activity on increased production and efficiency.

The trade union movement in the USA in its present form is comparatively modern, but its roots go deep. Originally the American Federation of Labor was composed of craft unions, and until President Roosevelt's New Deal of the early 1930s trade union organisation did not extend far outside that field. Part of the New Deal legislation emphasised the rights of trade unions to organise, and gave an opportunity for a new springboard of trade union organisation into a wider sphere.

This legislation provided that ballots about trade union membership could be taken in a factory, and two separate ballots could bring full union organisation as a result. The first ballot was to decide whether a union should be formed in the plant; the second was to decide which union. The development of mass production over many years had broken down craft skills and introduced more easily acquired skills, and had brought into being plants employing 5,000 workers and more. There was therefore a nucleus of former craft trade unionists in every plant who could use their persuasion on fellow-workers to join trade unions. Great propaganda campaigns were arranged by the unions, and one or two of the leaders of smaller craft unions saw an opportunity of increasing their spheres of influence. Accordingly, they linked up in a new body called first the Committee and later the Congress of Industrial Organisations to indicate that they too were going to organise on an industrial union basis.

Hard feelings developed between the two trade union bodies, the AFL and the CIO, but the immediate success of the latter made it a powerful force at the start. The Roosevelt administration was gleaming like a beacon of hope after the terrible years of depression, and the new hope and burning zeal of the political forces set the CIO campaign alight.

114

The new Automobile Workers' Union, its intention to organise every worker in the industry, ballooned in size, along with the Steelworkers. The Mineworkers' Union, too, grew swiftly for the unions now had a champion in Roosevelt and the backing of the law. This big surge forward of the United States trade union movement was due in part to the fierce reactionary opposition of some American employers, and also to the far-sighted policies of Roosevelt.

The highly individualist outlook of the American citizen reflects itself in their trade unions and although the AFL and the CIO came together in 1955 to form one centre, the AFL-CIO, some people were thinking before then that the days of the CIO as a separate organisation were limited.

The AFL-CIO is the only national trade union centre in the USA, but the Mineworkers have organisation in several other industries (the Lewis group) and are not in the AFL-CIO; nor are several of the railway unions and the United Automobile Workers. The Teamsters of America, a powerful union of $1\frac{1}{2}$ million members, was excluded by the AFL-CIO in 1959 for practices which were causing the name of trade unionism to be smirched.

There was a period in American trade unionism when gangsters and racketeers could have been a serious threat to some of the smaller unions but the bona fide central leadership fought them off, and in the main the gangsters and thugs were successful only at the fringes of some of the small unions. This was not a case of trade unions becoming corrupt; it was more a case of employers in some plants encouraging gangsters to form bogus 'unions' to keep the bona fide trade unions out; in other cases, gangsters deliberately formed groups of workers into so-called 'trade unions' to provide themselves with a regular income. To call a group 'a trade union' does not necessarily make it a trade union. Unfortunately, perhaps, there is no copyright in the term.

The AFL-CIO unions do an honest trade union job which is recognised by trade unionists anywhere; in a Press concerned with reporting the unusual or the abnormal it is natural that news of 'union' rackets, corruption, conspiracy and other evil methods should make headlines.

American citizens live in an individualistic society where the dollar sign is one of the recognised yardsticks of success. It is not surprising therefore that their organisations generally should adopt this test and trade unions in the USA can be no exception. Trade union leaders get remuneration more nearly on a par with that of industrialists; the members do not require their union leaders to be pointing the way to a new egalitarian society, because they believe that they already have such a society; certainly the American worker in general has no inhibitions about his equal place in the social scale, and he expects his trade union to concentrate its functions on getting him an extra two or three cents an hour from time to time, with shorter working hours or longer holidays with pay.

The agreements reached with the employers are legal contracts, usually for a two-year period. There is, in fact, a great deal more legal procedure in United States trade union matters and collective bargaining than there is in Britain, where there is virtually nil. It is unexpected to see that much of the rugged individualism of American trade unionism hinges on the law, and yet how little the law enters into industrial relations in 'law-abiding' Britain. No union in Britain consults a lawyer about the terms of a trade union agreement before they sign it, nor do they have that need. In the USA there is hardly a union agreement signed unless lawyers examine every word, every sentence, every comma. One movement uses lawyers, the other does not. Yet both are right, for each must do what it is necessary to do in each country's circumstances.

India's trade unions have their strength in the basic industries and are modelled on the British pattern. The Indian National Trade Union Congress has a membership of over $1\frac{3}{4}$ million and is strong in textiles, plantations, jute, steel, cement, sugar, transport and docks. It was formed in 1945. The Ahmedabad Textile Labour Association, however, was formed in 1923 and has a membership of 150,000. This Association has done great work for Indian trade unionism and continues to do so, many of the current leaders in various unions having been trained at some time or another in the Association. Many of the local leaders and workshop representatives are workers from the factories and mills.

The national leadership describe themselves as 'outsiders'—that is, they come from outside the industry. They are dedicated men, living austere lives, who have left their professions and scholastic careers in order to devote their lives to raising the material, cultural and spiritual standards of working people. They are realists and enthusiasts, not cranks. These leaders are impressive.

There is another smaller centre, the Hind Mazdoor Sabha, whose headquarters are in Bombay, which has the support of as good a dock workers' union as could be found in most parts of Europe. The aims and objects of INTUC and HMS are similar and the differences between them are mainly political, and there are indications that closer organisational links might develop between the two organisations.

The Communist Party sponsors a trade union movement called the All-India Trades Union Congress which makes its main drive into the newer, expanding general and electrical engineering industries and steel, but both the INTUC and HMS are aware of these political implications and the dangers of this to the nation. Ideological differences between the Communist Party of India and the Communist Party (Marxist) were reflected in AITUC which split as a Communist Party (Marxist) faction setting up the Centre of Indian Trade Unions. Another organisation, the United Trade Union Congress, has a membership of about 100,000, but there are also a great number of unattached trade unions, many of them small and insignificant, which in time may become merged in the bigger federations which constitute the INTUC.

The process of collective bargaining in India in its later stages, that is conciliation and arbitration, is subject to extensive legal procedures and many employers force the unions through the lengthy legal process. Twelve months or more may elapse between claim and settlement. For hungry people this is a long time to wait. The communist AITUC makes quick settlements with the employers for a lower increase than either HMS or INTUC would countenance. Some short-sighted employers therefore encourage the communist AITUC and say, with incredible naïvety, that AITUC 'controls its members better'.

This relationship between the communist organisation and the most reactionary employers is easily understandable. The AITUC gets an inadequate settlement but it is a quick 'something'. The reactionary employer pays a smaller increase than would be accepted by either INTUC or HMS. The result is that the employer makes a bigger profit and the AITUC gets support from some working people on the grounds that it gets quick results, although they may be small. The democratic forces in India are thus the losers and it is the reactionary elements who gain.

As the Indian standard of living improves and industries are more firmly on their feet with transport and communications better, the political and economic self-restraints, exercised very tightly still, will relax and the division between INTUC and HMS will narrow. This should make for a more unified trade union movement, for there is no fundamental difference in the aims of either. So far as AITUC is concerned, the rising standard of living in India will cause its influence to diminish.

The trade union movement in Malaysia is another movement successfully based on a British pattern of organisation. Its leadership is modest and mature and solidly backed by the membership. The Malaysian Trades Union Congress has no rival centre and its policies and those of all its unions are formulated on an economic basis with no organisational commitment to any political party. Its representations are made direct to government, and it contrives to keep legal processes to the minimum, direct negotiations and settlements being effected at every point.

Its biggest affiliated union, with about 120,000 members, is the National Union of Plantation Workers, with a fine headquarters building in Selangor and a newspaper printed in three languages. This union is outstanding in every way, and despite the fact that it began to be formed as recently as 1946 it will stand comparison with most unions anywhere in the world.

The Japanese trade union movement has two national centres, SOHYO and DOMEI, the former having the bigger membership. The differences here are political; DOMEI, an anti-communist trade union federation, alleges that SOHYO is either 'fellow-traveller' or communist-dominated, which SOHYO denies. Both organisations certainly devote a great deal of time to political representations and there is a strong theoretical approach to industrial relations.

Again, the Japanese historic, economic and political background must be taken into account in reviewing SOHYO's activities, for unions, being made up of people, cannot do other than reflect the minds of people. There is little doubt that the Japanese Socialist Party, tiny in membership, is a formidable force in Parliament only as a result of the political and financial support it receives from some of the unions; the Liberal Democratic

Party relies for its finance on individual employers and support from business firms.

The German trade union movement (DGB) was catastrophically affected during the course of its history by national political events and had to re-organise itself completely after 1945. For example, in 1933 virtually the first action which Hitler took was to destroy the German trade union movement.

Mussolini, too, had previously eliminated the democratically-controlled Italian trade unions and replaced them with Fascist organisations.

In Spain also the bona fide unions had been immediately liquidated. Totalitarian forces, when they have gained power do not dare to let bona fide trade unions continue their existence, and their first onslaught invariably is directed against them. Bona fide trade unionism and totalitarianism are incompatible. They cannot exist together at the same time in any country.

The suppression of independent trade unionism by a dictatorship is followed by that dictatorship establishing so-called trade unions which are not controlled by the workers but which are used as propaganda agencies by the regime and also for certain social welfare work. Not at any point are they allowed to be a means for the full expression of workers' views or as independent bodies for the purpose of collective bargaining.

Today, the German trade union movement has over 6 million members organised on the principles of industrial trade unionism. Its sixteen trade unions cater for every kind of worker, but nevertheless a separate organisation for non-manual workers generally exists outside the ranks of the DGB.

In France, there are three trade union centres, the communist-dominated Confederation Général du Travail (CGT), the Force Ouvrière (FO) and the Confédération Française Démocratique du Travail (CFDT) formerly the Confédération Française des Travailleurs Chrétiens.

In actual affiliations, none are strong in relation to the industrial population of France: they are all influential in action. The French trade union movement is really a vast congregation of small independent units which give little support to national trade union administration or policy.

In Italy there are three trade union centres, Catholic, socialist and communist; in Jugoslavia, a near neighbour, one centre exists for a movement based on industrial unionism operating very closely with the ruling political party. Sweden and Israel provide other examples of the close co-operation of trade union centres with government and political party, but there are great differences between these two, and even greater differences between them both and the movement in Jugoslavia.

In Latin-American countries changes of government and regimes can take place overnight by means of coups: democratic procedures for the election of governments are often by-passed. In Venezuela, where a democratic republic has replaced many years of dictatorships, the swiftly-growing trade union movement is making an enormous contribution to a new national stability which the democratic government recognises fully. The republic-wide Confederacion de Trabajadores de Venezuela with a claimed membership of 1,300,000 is based on national industrial federations composed of local branches. The oil workers, with about 60,000 members, the transport workers, and the construction workers are strong bulwarks of the CTV.

In addition, the CTV draws strength and support from the State, or regional, federations which are composed of all the unions in the several states which make up the Republic. As industry develops and road and rail communications improve, the other national federations will become more closely knit, and in that process will play a most important role in the Republic's economic, social and political development. The CTV may well set a new pattern for democratic advance in the whole of the continent.

It is well to note from this examination of various trade union movements that there is no strict formula of organisation or operation on which all trade unions can be unanimous; but all will claim that their objective is to improve the living standards of their members. How they do it, and when they do it, is a decision which is not solely within the control of trade unions. Trade unions can help to create circumstances which may be favourable for their objectives, but they cannot decide the circumstances. Other functions and other bodies also enter into the picture. A trade union movement therefore must do what it can, when it can and how it can, in the circumstances and environment in which it works; since those circumstances are changing all the time and at a faster rate usually than environments, it cannot have a fixed theory or dogma to meet all circumstances. It needs to be flexible in its views, free in its operation.

The star on the horizon gives little light to show the pitfalls and obstacles under foot; even the star itself may vanish behind the clouds from time to time. The union however must continue to struggle along, taking its members with it. Political parties come and go, party leaders change, individuals vanish from the scene. The aim of the union must be constant; its function must be independent and within the control only of its members, acting within the general law.

14

Trade Unions and the Future

DEMOCRATIC trade unionism is in the world to stay. Its usefulness will remain unchanged, but its methods will change according to the changing circumstances in which each national trade union movement works.

The broad, unchanging, general objective of a trade union movement is to improve the economic and social conditions of workers in all parts of the world and to render them assistance, whether such workers are employed or have ceased to be employed. This general objective is wide enough to cover all aspects of the future work of trade unionism.

Under such an umbrella the variety and volume of trade union work are bound to alter. As industry changes and needs more technicians, more skilled workpeople and fewer less-skilled, the manual unions will change their form and status; new trade unions will come into existence, too, to cover workpeople who formerly were thought to be averse to trade union organisation. The status which improving educational standards will bring will lessen social gaps and, as a society moves away from two nations within a nation to one nation as a whole, conflict between management and workpeople will diminish.

All over the world the ownership of industry is passing from the small proprietor to public companies under the direction of professional managers and salaried employees. Their livelihoods, although of a different standard, are dependent on their earnings in the same way that workpeople are at present dependent on their hourly rates and their weekly wages. The inheritance of businesses, and therefore the handing down from father to son of managerial power, is also diminishing and the door to top management functions will become more open to the appointment of the men with the most ability. These new men, as modern democracy develops its social and educational advance, are more likely to be drawn from the families of workpeople in the future than is the case at present.

In other cases the economic and social needs of a nation will call for the national ownership of particular industries or their public control. The high cost of new and complicated machinery for mass production to satisfy the growing needs of developing countries and the rapid expansion of their living standards will be beyond the reach of the smaller manufacturing units or the small-holder in agriculture.

Growing technical research will require more and better-educated personnel and this can only be met on the scale required by improved and more extensive educational systems. The moves towards social equality, based on educational opportunity, will accelerate. Trade unions themselves will be a moving force in this direction and will themselves be affected by the results.

There will be less need for oratory and mass meetings in trade unions and more need for books and periodicals, a greater need for argument and logic rather than rhetoric. Injustice in society will be less obvious but none the less real, and it will be towards the perception, prevention and cure of this that trade unions will move.

Poverty is relative. It can be defined as being without bread and shoes and shelter. In another country it means being unable to afford a radio or a television. The shortages of material things can be overcome relatively quickly in a modern scientific society. Mental poverty, because it does not bring a physical pain or a pressing feeling of want, is harder to overcome.

In the same way that industries change, and people's outlooks change, trade unions will change also; but conscious change in anticipation of events calls for planning. The day-to-day, bread-and-butter work of trade unions of the future will continue, but leaders of workpeople, the wage-earners and salary-earners, need to be in the advance of modern thinking. Planners, research workers, statisticians and accountants, production experts and men of wide general knowledge and experience to assess future trends in the economy, will be used by unions, ultimately if they are not already, to match up with management and government experts.

The leadership must be equipped to check and measure the trends and possibilities of production and distribution; to ensure, so far as they can, that the new society does not develop into a technocracy still based on privilege for the few, even though qualifications different from the old proprietorship will be necessary to ensure such privilege.

Governments will become more involved with industry. New and developing society will call for new towns, and the provision of houses, factories, shops, schools, hospitals and roads, sanitation and social security measures will require a bigger national budget. Local authorities, too, will look towards industry as well as individuals for the provision of the revenue to supply other communal needs.

In helping to establish this new society trade unions will widen their function and make alterations in their structure and services to their members. The work of some small unions, limited as it is to the workpeople employed in one single factory, may be effective at present, but when the factory becomes part of a combine, where other unions have already organised, arrangements will have to be made as early as possible either to federate or amalgamate. The centre of management will have moved, and the relationship of individual employees to management will become more remote. The day when an employer could say that he knew every workman by name has either vanished or is on its last legs everywhere

The federations which small unions may eventually form should not be confined to conferences, consultations and negotiations. The federations must be more than mere convening bodies; they must be able, within a short time, to transform themselves into national unions, able to develop on behalf of all their members the educational, organisational and research facilities capable of dealing with modern industrial problems. And able to exercise a central authority.

They will need to have special machinery within them to deal with the specific requirements of the membership, providing separate sections for separate interests, the one common factor binding the members being the common relationship of employment in the same industry or related trades. It would be foolish not to recognise that distinctions exist in a common employment, as between skilled, semi-skilled, production, administrative and clerical workers.

The federations, or amalgamated unions, so formed will also need to have a strong common link. The concerted actions of managements and the decisions taken by governments in the field of industrial and social developments will have a common application and effect on workers in the oil industry as well as the sugar industry, the distributive trades, and all the rest. Therefore there must be a strong central body of all the unions to initiate common action in the interests of them all. This central body must be provided by the unions with the financial resources to enable it to function effectively in their common interests.

The low contributions which some trade unions receive from their members may make it impossible to give the amount of service which the leadership knows the members should have to face the economic development of the time: a union leadership which is not prepared to call on the members to pay an adequate amount for a proper service should leave the field. An impoverished, inadequate union will only be an obstacle, blocking the way for others or impeding the establishment of a new body which would be up to date in structure and outlook.

National centres themselves will need to develop closer contact with regional and world organisations of trade unions in order to make their full impact on those organisations which make decisions related to the political and economic requirements of mankind. The World Monetary Fund, the United Nations, the International Labour Organisation are examples. The trade union voice must be heard there just as much as in every factory. Trade unions should develop as a positive spur for research and technical advance in industry, for national economic and social development and international planning.

No question arises about whether trade unions will be stronger in the future than they are now. They will be. That is inevitable. The question is not whether their growing influence will be for the good of industries and nations; their work will inevitably make that contribution. The real question is whether the impact of trade unionism on the future of the world will be as effective and speedy as it could be.

The answer to that is not a matter for final judgment now, but it is a question of faith for the future. An answer, however, can be given. If trade union purpose is properly understood, if the effort of the early trade unionists for economic advance and universal social justice can be duplicated now and in the future, then the answer is an emphatic affirmative.